DATE		

The Bill of Rights

Also by Milton Meltzer

Voices from the Civil War:
A Documentary History of the Great American Conflict

The American Revolutionaries:
A History in Their Own Words 1750–1800

Rescue: *The Story of How Gentiles
Saved Jews in the Holocaust*

Never to Forget:
The Jews of the Holocaust

Ain't Gonna Study War No More:
The Story of America's Peace Seekers

Starting from Home:
A Writer's Beginnings

The Landscape of Memory

Poverty in America

Benjamin Franklin:
The New American

George Washington and the Birth of Our Nation

Langston Hughes:
A Biography

Mark Twain:
A Writer's Life

All Times, All Peoples:
A World History of Slavery

The Terrorists

The Black Americans:
A History in Their Own Words

The Jewish Americans:
A History in Their Own Words

The Hispanic Americans

The Chinese Americans

The Bill of Rights

HOW WE GOT IT
AND WHAT IT MEANS

MILTON MELTZER

THOMAS Y. CROWELL

NEW YORK

Printed in the United States of America. For information address
Thomas Y. Crowell Junior Books, 10 East 53rd Street, New York,
NY 10022.
1 2 3 4 5 6 7 8 9 10
First Edition

Library of Congress Cataloging-in-Publication Data
Meltzer, Milton, date
    The Bill of Rights : how we got it and what it means / by Milton
Meltzer.
        p.   cm.
    Includes bibliographical references.
    Summary: Traces the history of the Bill of Rights included in the
United States' Constitution and highlights contemporary challenges
to each of the ten amendments.
    ISBN 0-690-04805-X. — ISBN 0-690-04807-6 (lib. bdg.)
    1. Civil rights—United States—Juvenile literature.   2. United
States—Constitutional law—Amendments—1st-10th—Juvenile
literature.   3. United States—Constitutional history—Juvenile
literature.   [1. Civil rights.   2. United States—Constitutional
law—Amendments—1st-10th.   3. United States—Constitutional
history.]   I. Title.
KF4750.M45   1990   90-1537
342.73'085—dc20   CIP
[347.30285]   AC

ABQ1721

For Estelle and Emanuel Margolis

CONTENTS

	Foreword	ix
1	The Ancient Cry for Liberty	1
2	A Startling Leap Forward	10
3	The Spark of Resistance	22
4	Treading on Enchanted Ground	28
5	Liberty Won: How Preserve It?	34
6	What the People Are Entitled To	48
7	The Ten Amendments	55
8	If There Is Any Fixed Star	66
9	The Right to Dissent	73
10	Freedom—and the Witch-Hunt	84
11	Secrecy and Censorship	96
12	A Nation of Joiners	108
13	Gun Control	115

14 The Right to Be Let Alone   121

15 The Right to Remain Silent   129

16 The Promise of a Fair Trial   136

17 The Law Should Be Humane   145

18 Powers that Belong to the People   153

    Afterword   159

    Time Line   162

    Note on Sources   165

    Bibliography   167

    General Background   171

    Index   175

FOREWORD

Do you know what's in the Bill of Rights?

It may sound like a foolish question. Many Americans automatically claim they revere this document and believe deeply in the wisdom of the Founding Fathers who conceived it. Yet, when they are asked by opinion pollsters to tell what the major provisions of the Bill of Rights are, they rarely get it right. For some fifty years now the Gallup and other polls have made surveys of public opinion on this question. The results are astonishing—and sad. A large percentage of those queried have only the vaguest notion of the historic document. Worse, when the pollsters put into somewhat different words the essence of each of those rights, an alarming percentage of people say they disapprove of those rights!

Try it out for yourself: See if you can jot down at least some of the rights guaranteed us by the first ten amendments to the Constitution. Then check your memory against the text of the Bill, printed on pages 55–63.

Let's go at it another way. Suppose the Bill of Rights didn't exist. What could happen to you without its protection?

- You publicly criticize the president, or you picket the White House, and you land in jail.

- The Congress decides to make a particular religion the official one and you, who believe in a different faith, are not allowed to practice it.

- You sign a petition, or attend a meeting to protest some government action, and the police arrest you for it.

- You are accused of breaking a law and are arrested. But you are not allowed to consult a lawyer, you are held in jail indefinitely with bail denied you, and when the case comes up, your guilt or innocence is determined without a lawyer in court to defend you, and without a jury of your peers to judge you.

- If you are convicted of a crime, there is no limit on the nature of your punishment. It can be as cruel as the court and your jailers wish.

- Any property you own can be taken away from you, without compensation, by the local, state, or federal government whenever they say that property is needed for some public purpose.

• The police, without any warrant, can enter your home at any time of day or night to search your possessions and take whatever they choose.

This is by no means all that could happen to you. But it's enough to suggest how defenseless, and how helpless, we would be without the protection of the Bill of Rights.

Let's suppose you say, I'm the kind of person who never gets into trouble. I mind my own business, I never complain or criticize, and of course I would never commit a crime. Perhaps true, but what if you are falsely accused of committing one? What would help protect you from a miscarriage of justice?

Remember, you are a citizen. And in a democracy citizens should vote. To vote intelligently you need to hear all sides of public issues. The Bill of Rights tries to make sure that voices on any side of a controversy will not be silenced. Otherwise you would not be able to know what dissenters think so that you can decide for yourself the truth or merit of a belief or a political position. So even the passive or inactive person needs the Bill of Rights.

How and why did these rights come into being? What did they mean to the Americans of two centuries ago? Why is this cornerstone of our democracy constantly being tested? Have we ever lost any of our rights? Could we lose them now?

This book will explore these questions. In the first part of the book (chapters 1–6) we'll look into the historical circumstances that led to the creation of a bill of rights. It doesn't help to set the Founding

Fathers on a pedestal, like demigods, or to think of the Constitution with its Bill of Rights as a sacred document. It was born of historical forces and conflicting interests. I will try to make these clear. Chapter 7 gives the text of the Bill of Rights, with a brief explanation of the meaning of each of the ten amendments. Chapters 8 through 18 describe some of the ways in which the Bill of Rights has been interpreted and applied down through the years. A deeper sense of this history will help us find our way into the future.

1
THE ANCIENT CRY
FOR LIBERTY

Hardly a day goes by without some story appearing in the newspapers about civil liberties. An angry parent demands that certain young-adult novels be removed from the school library shelves because they are obscene. A black immigrant from Jamaica takes a landlord to court because he has been refused the rental of an apartment. From his prison cell an inmate protests that he was not given a fair trial. The head of a rifle club opposes a law that would limit the members' right to bear arms. A witness pleads his right to remain silent when summoned to testify before a Senate investigating committee. A woman arrested on a minor charge assails the judge because he has set unreasonable bail.

All these stories are part of the continuing struggle to maintain both liberty and order in a democratic society. Seeing how tightly the Bill of Rights is woven into the fabric of our daily lives, it is easy to realize that the Constitution would not have been adopted some 200 years ago if the Founding Fathers had not promised to add a Bill of Rights.

The Constitution was written in Philadelphia in the summer of 1787. The delegates threw aside the old Articles of Confederation that had loosely linked the original thirteen colonies for six years and came up with a radically new plan of government that had to be approved by the states.

Even before the first ratifying convention met, a clamor rose from every quarter of the new nation for a specific Bill of Rights. We demand a guarantee of personal freedoms, cried the people, and we want this safeguard against tyranny put in writing.

Was the idea of a Bill of Rights something new? Out of what human experience did that cry for rights come? The makers of constitutions work from a historical mold. For what others have done in the past, even the most remote past, shapes what is done now. What worked, what failed, and why, are considered by minds seeking to pluck the fruits of history to meet present needs.

It was Congressman James Madison of Virginia who wrote the first draft of the ten amendments that became the Bill of Rights. His draft became the substance of the final version. But he did not dream it up out of his imagination. The ideas, even many of the phrases, were the logical outcome of what had happened before in the struggles for freedom both in England and in the American colonies. The federal Bill of Rights is based directly upon the great charters of English liberty. And these began with the Magna Carta. Without that English precedent, it is doubtful that the American revolutionaries could have done what they did when they framed our Bill of Rights.

The year of the Magna Carta, 1215, is celebrated as a great milestone on the road to liberty and due process of law. It was the time when the discontented English barons forced King John to give them a guarantee that he would govern more reasonably. On a meadow called Runnymede, John agreed to put his seal to the Magna Carta. The great charter was drawn up after extensive talks among the king, the rebel barons, and the archbishop of Canterbury. It was a grant, in sixty-three clauses, of certain rights and privileges that the king pledged to observe. No longer would the monarchy be despotic. By defining the law, the charter limited the king's power. The primary aim of the barons was to protect their own interests. But because they needed support outside their class, they provided for dealing with other people's interests too.

How fundamental the Magna Carta was can be seen from this important clause:

No freeman shall be taken or imprisoned or be disseized of his freehold, or liberties, or free customs, or be outlawed, or exiled, or any other wise destroyed, nor will we pass upon him, nor condemn him, but by lawful judgment of his peers, or by the law of the land.

". . . the law of the land. . . ." Exactly what this was, was not defined. But there *was* a law; this the charter says very strongly. And law means recognized procedures, procedures even a king must follow.

So in the Magna Carta can be found the root of the

principle that there are fundamental laws *above* the state. And the state, though it otherwise has sovereign power, may not infringe upon those fundamental rights. Although the Magna Carta is phrased in a feudal form that makes it sound like a gift from the king, the reality was different, and everyone knew it. The promises made at Runnymede were forced from His Majesty by nobles—and their enemies—in the cause of preserving their power in their own parts of the kingdom.

While the Magna Carta was a document directed at specific feudal abuses committed by the king, its key parts are phrased more broadly. This made it possible in later centuries to interpret them as precedents toward establishing liberties we now consider basic. For example, in the passage cited above, originally the words "no baron" were used, but then changed to "no freeman." That change was of great importance. It made the charter broad enough to protect the whole nation against governmental oppression.

Over the centuries two parts of the Great Charter came to be seen as the most vital. One is the principle that it is the nation itself that has the only right to ordain taxation. And the other is read as a guarantee, to all men, of trial by jury, absolutely barring arbitrary arrest, and as a pledge to provide to everyone full, free, and speedy justice—equally to all. In the phrase quoted above—"by the law of the land"—is found the powerful link to the "due process of law" which is at the heart of the American Bill of Rights.

Although it was not the barons' intent in 1215 to draft the words of the Magna Carta in such a way that they could be made to serve the needs of other times, unwittingly they did. The charter became a sacred text to the English. It was a steady source of tradition and strength in the fight to rein in the despots of later days. Its principles crossed the ocean and were cited by the American colonists as they asserted their rights against the English authority of the eighteenth century.

A second great English precedent for the American Bill of Rights came some four hundred years after the Magna Carta. It was the Petition of Right of 1628. (Note that this was only a few years after the Pilgrims landed at Plymouth Rock.) Sir Edward Coke, a great English lawyer and writer, was the central force for the petition. Once the highest judge in the realm, Coke was removed because he tried to frustrate royal attempts to raise the power of the Crown above the law. Then, at the age of 65, Coke was elected to the House of Commons. He became the parliamentary leader of the opposition to the Crown. Charles I, who had been on the throne only a few years, began launching attacks upon the personal liberties of the people. He forced loans from them and punished those who refused to pay. He billeted soldiers in private homes, and at his personal whim sent men to prison without trial.

In revolt against such arbitrary rule, Coke led the 1628 Commons to adopt the Petition of Right as a law declaring the fundamental rights of Englishmen. In the next century, across the ocean, Coke's courage and initiative would inspire such revolutionaries as James Otis, Patrick Henry, and John Adams.

The conflict between the Crown and Parliament led ultimately to the English Revolution that toppled Charles I. In 1649, rebel army leaders sketched out a constitution for a republican government; it was known as the Agreement of the People. The document was a landmark in the history of constitutional theory. With Charles I gone from the throne (and soon to be executed), the English wanted a written constitution that would define limits upon the power of government. Limits the Parliament itself could not violate.

The Agreement of the People specified matters the Parliament should not be able to alter, including freedom of religion (except for Catholics) and equality before the law. Soon the agreement was quietly set aside and another constitution adopted in 1653. But it was without any real limits upon the parliamentary government.

Nevertheless, ideas about government and limits upon its power, which were hotly debated in these years of ferment, would later be important to the framers of the American Constitution. They learned that it wasn't enough to declare fundamental rights and limits in a constitution. You also had to include the machinery to enforce such provisions. No such machinery was provided in these early English attempts.

Another great step forward was taken in 1656 with the publication of a pamphlet by a remarkable man who helped overthrow Charles I. He was Sir Henry Vane, an early leader of the Commonwealth government. In "A Healing Question," Vane proposed that a constitution be drawn up by a convention of the people, called together for that very purpose. He was making a distinction between what legislatures ordinarily do and the special and unique function of a constitutional convention. His idea was exactly what the Americans would follow during the Revolution, when representatives of the newly independent states would write the Constitution and Bill of Rights.

A long series of royal abuses was brought to a halt by the Puritan Revolution in England. The "left wing" of the period—they were called the Levellers—wanted to make the people's liberties more secure by getting a constitution down on paper, where all could read it. This attempt failed, but popular feeling against arbitrary government mounted high enough for a Bill of Rights to emerge in 1689. This act of Parliament became the supreme law of the land. It embodied the basic principles of liberty as the English then understood them.

The 1689 Bill of Rights declared these things *unconstitutional:*

- the suspension of acts of Parliament

- the levying of taxes without the consent of Parliament

- the maintenance of a standing army in time of peace

- the interference with free elections

- the infliction of cruel and unusual punishment
- the exaction of excessive bail
- the denial of the right of petition

But just as important as the issue of political liberty was the struggle for religious freedom in England. In fact, it was religious strife that intensified the political differences and brought about the civil war that overthrew the royal family of the Stuarts. Heretics—people who held religious opinions opposed to the authorized beliefs—had long been hounded in England, their writings outlawed, and the teaching of their beliefs bringing jail and loss of property. In 1401 Parliament had gone further, making heresy a capital crime and authorizing the burning of heretics. King, Parliament, and church had joined in introducing the Inquisition to England. Some fifty heretics went to the stake between 1401 and 1534, before Parliament repealed the heretic-burning law. Many more suffered lesser punishments as thousands of early Protestants were put to the Inquisition.

Most of the English at that time believed the state had the duty "to uphold truth and repress error"—and whether Protestant or Catholic was in power, they carried out that duty. It was the victims of that dictation over religion who were among those who left England beginning in the seventeenth century to settle in the American colonies. Many came in the hope of living better in America, in worshipping as they pleased.

But at the same time the English adopted the 1689

Bill of Rights, they also passed a Toleration Act. The Church of England was still the state church, the official church. But a number of Protestant sects had split off from it. The Toleration Act was a step toward freedom of religion, giving the people some religious concessions and legalizing the worship of Protestant nonconformists. Roman Catholics, however, did not benefit from the act.

In the century to come, the American revolutionaries would draw up their own declarations of rights. From the English model they took the name Bill of Rights and often the very phrasing of the English law.

2

A STARTLING LEAP FORWARD

The first charter issued to an American colony—Virginia, in 1606—provided that the colonists and their descendants were to "have and enjoy all liberties, franchises, and immunities . . . as if they had been abiding and born, within this our Realm of England . . ."

That fact—that these were British colonies—is important to remember in thinking about the Bill of Rights. For the colonies settled by Great Britain were vastly different from those settled by Spain or France, whose legal traditions were not at all the same. When the English migrated, they packed along with their worldly goods basic concepts of English law and liberty.

Let's pause to see who the colonists were. By 1750 they numbered about 1.5 million. The last sizeable groups of English settlers had arrived fifty years earlier. The people who came in the 1700s far outnumbered the English. They were mainly from Ireland,

Germany, Switzerland, and Africa. It's likely that half of all the white people who came were indentured servants. They were so poor that they had no way to pay the cost of the voyage. To obtain passage, they signed a contract, called articles of indenture, which bound them to servitude for from four to seven years. When their terms were up, many of these people started their lives anew somewhere on the frontier. They were hardworking people, intent on becoming self-sufficient. They built their own homes, raised their own food, and made their own clothes. Father and mother worked equally hard, their children pitching in from an early age to help the family make a go of it.

But there never were enough of these white working people to meet the needs of employers. They turned to another source of labor, the people of Africa. They bought or kidnapped Africans to work as slaves on the plantations of the south or as domestic servants in the north. By 1750 there were more than 300,000 black people in the colonies, or about one fifth of the population.

That population included, of course, the Indians, or Native Americans. They had lived on this land for thousands of years. More and more settlers moved in with guns and axes and plows; the Indians watched, despairing as the forests were chopped down, the animals killed, the fields cleared. Some of the Indians escaped westward; others resisted, hoping futilely to drive the invaders out.

The colonists drew upon the institutions and ideas they had brought with them. These were naturally

English, because it was the English who founded the colonies and it was English charters, governors, and laws that controlled them. In the mother country it was commonly accepted that the aim of government was to protect life, property, and liberty. Without such protection, most people believed that the greedy and the cruel would make victims of everyone else. No longer would life, property, and liberty be safe.

But government is not an abstraction. It is made up of people. The question of who makes the decisions of government is crucial to any society. In England, people no longer believed in the divine right of kings to do as they pleased. That outmoded idea of God-given authority had been replaced by the belief that government must balance the interests of all classes of society. At the time of colonization this meant the monarchy, the aristocracy, and the ordinary people. A good government would restrain each of these three, to prevent any one of them from overwhelming the others. Otherwise, a king could become a tyrant, the aristocracy could become a corrupt oligarchy, and the people could fall into anarchy or mob rule.

Behind this thinking was the fear of governmental power. A good government would use power to do good; a bad one, to do harm. As the colonies moved into the eighteenth century, most people had come to believe that too much power permitted to any person or group was sure to bring on corruption and tyranny.

What was the structure of the colonial governments? At the top was a governor. He was the king's agent. Then came the legislature, usually in the form of two houses. The upper house, called the council, made up of the well-to-do, was commonly appointed by the governor. The lower house, called the assembly, was elected by the white male freeholders. The upper house spoke for the aristocracy; the lower, for the people. But not all the people: only adult white males with enough property to produce a certain annual rental income could vote and be elected to office. All other white males were excluded. And so were all women, all blacks, all Indians, and all non-Christians. These people were considered to be so ignorant or poor or unpredictable that they could not cast a thoughtful vote or make a responsible decision.

When we talk about government then, we are talking about the decisions made by a markedly limited group of people, an elite. The others, however, did not hesitate to holler when they thought those who ruled them did wrong. They wanted justice and freedom, heckled their leaders, organized protests, and even rose up in arms when abuses became intolerable.

The colonial charters that came from London could be amended or revoked at will by the grantors. The grantors regulated the lives and property of the colonists. When the colonists began to write their own basic laws, these too were legally subject to the supreme authority of the British government. Most Americans, however, came to see it differently. As John Adams put it, the very first charter, of James I to Virginia, "is more like a treaty between independent sovereigns than like a charter or grant of privileges from sovereign to his subjects."

The Americans regarded their charters as the solid rock upon which their rights and liberties stood. When attempts were made by London to restrict or modify those rights, the colonial legislatures resisted loudly. They saw themselves as direct descendants of the House of Commons. All the privileges and powers that legislatures had won in the struggle against royal absolutism were now theirs, too.

Inevitably that vision of self-government threw the popular assemblies into head-on clashes with the royal governors who believed they were not beholden to those they governed. Gradually, though, the privileges Parliament had won for itself—such as control over its own procedure and freedom of debate—were gained by the colonial legislatures. So too was the vitally important power of the purse—control over the colonies' own finances.

That first document creating the earliest English settlement—the Virginia Charter of 1606—established a great precedent. It stated that the colonists were entitled to all the "rights of Englishmen." The same guarantee was repeated in the charters of New England, Massachusetts Bay, Maryland, Connecticut, Rhode Island, Carolina, and Georgia.

The Virginia Charter (granted when Shakespeare was still writing his plays) was a first step toward our own federal Bill of Rights. Only a first step, of course, for it did nothing to make sure that those rights would be implemented.

Precisely what those "rights of Englishmen" were, the charter did not define. It couldn't have, really, for it would take the constitutional struggles of the seventeenth and eighteenth centuries in England to bring the vague concept of fundamental rights down to earth. We've already noted the great steps forward in England that followed the Magna Carta—the Petition of Rights, the Agreement of the People, the Bill of Rights. What would shape movement within the colonies toward an American Bill of Rights?

It was the settlers themselves, through their elected legislatures, who went beyond the bare generality to give rights a specific content. They did this by passing laws that tried to define the rights colonists were entitled to. Maryland was the first to move, through an Act of 1639, which provided that no colonist could be imprisoned or have his property taken or be exiled except "according to the law of this Province." That phrase, stemming from the Magna Carta, anticipated the due process clause found in modern American constitutions.

Going far beyond the voicing of one principle, Massachusetts in 1641 enacted the first detailed American Charter of Liberties. Considering its early date, it was an amazing document to come out of so young a colony. Massachusetts Bay Colony was founded at Boston in 1630 by Puritans who hoped to establish in the New World an ideal commonwealth in which their "purified" church could prosper. With them they brought a charter from Charles I, which soon became a constitution for the colony. By 1640 more than 25,000 refugees were making their home in Massachusetts, now the largest of the English settlements in America.

The Puritan leaders were interested neither in freedom of worship for others nor in a free system of government. "Democracy," patriarch John Cotton said, was "not fit government either for church or commonwealth." But the town meetings soon rebelled against the rigid rule of the church fathers. Under pressure from the settlers, the Puritans appointed the Reverend Nathaniel Ward of Ipswich to draw up the Massachusetts Body of Liberties. Ward not only was a minister, but also had studied law and practiced in the English common law courts. After full debate in town meeting and in the legislature, the law code was adopted by the General Court. It dealt with matters of religion—providing capital punishment for those who refused to profess faith in God—as well as secular questions of land, trade, and property. But the document's greatest importance was its restatement of certain individual rights and liberties whose origins lay as far back as the Magna Carta.

The document is the most important forerunner of the federal Bill of Rights. Harsh and narrow-minded as the Puritans were by modern standards, they still were able to replace a religious oligarchy with a representative system of government. The people wanted their rights set down in black and white, so they would not be at the mercy of any high-handed authority. The document was molded not only by such precedents as the Magna Carta, but also by the experience in self-government of the colonists themselves. Scholars call the Massachusetts Body of Liberties a "startling" leap forward.

Among the guarantees it protected were freedom of speech and assembly in public meetings, equal protection under the laws, just compensation for private property taken for public use, freedom to emigrate, the right to bail, the right to employ counsel, trial by jury in civil cases, the right to challenge jurors, restrictions on imprisonment for debt, speedy trial, no double jeopardy, and no cruel or excessive punishments.

It also protected some of the rights of women, children, servants, aliens, and even animals, and went so far as to outlaw slavery as well. Note too that it recognized that one's liberty depended, in the last resort, upon the courts. We can take the federal Bill of Rights and match many of its parts with sections of this document created 150 years earlier.

It was both the desire for economic gain and the flight from religious persecution that led the English to plant colonies in the strange new world. But the fact that many English colonists came to escape religious persecution did not at all mean they were tolerant of religious practices different from their own. Sadly, when those once persecuted by the Church of England won control of colonial governments, they switched from oppressed to oppressors. Only *their* beliefs were right, and they demanded that all others follow them, or be condemned as heretics.

In a few colonies, however, religious persecution was not allowed. Maryland and Rhode Island were actually founded as refuges of toleration. Maryland's patron was the first Lord Baltimore, who wanted his colony to become a haven for Catholics like himself. Knowing he would need other colonists too, he opened the door to Protestants. In 1649, Maryland adopted an Act Concerning Religion that gave all Christians—Catholic and Protestant alike—freedom of conscience and worship. While protection was limited to Christians, there is no evidence that Jews or others were persecuted in the colony. Maryland thus became the first colony to recognize a measure of freedom of conscience. Maryland's phrase—"the free exercise of religion"—would be absorbed into the first clause of the federal Bill of Rights.

Important as this pioneering measure was, it was still an act of the legislature, and therefore could be repealed by it. It was Roger Williams's Rhode Island, in 1663, that carried the idea forward, making the doctrine of religious liberty fundamental law by placing it within its charter itself.

Young Roger Williams was a Puritan minister who left his native England when the government made life for religious dissenters too miserable to endure. Arriving in Boston in 1631, Williams found the Massachusetts authorities just as hostile to dissent. Williams maintained the "strange opinion" that civil government should have no power in spiritual matters. From this heretical attack upon the alliance of church and state, Williams moved into the political realm, charging that King James had no right to give grants and patents to land that belonged to the Indians. Tried in 1635 as a dangerous agitator, he was banished from the colony.

Williams fled to Rhode Island where tolerant Indians offered him sanctuary, and founded the settlement at Providence. He made toleration the cornerstone of the new colony of Rhode Island. Even

Quakers and Jews were allowed to worship as they wished. In 1663 the colony secured a royal charter from Charles II. It had the status of a constitution and remained in force until 1842, long after the Revolution. The charter built religious liberty into American constitutional law. It declared, in broad language, that "no person within the said colony, at any time hereafter, shall be any wise molested, punished, disquieted, or called in question, for any difference in opinion in matters of religion," so long as he did "not actually disturb the civil peace of our said colony." And further, that this guarantee was to prevail, "any law, statute or clause . . . usage or custom of this realm, to the contrary hereof, in any wise, not withstanding."

The next expansion of personal freedom came through the Charter of Fundamental Law of West New Jersey in 1677. Drafted probably by William Penn, one of the proprietors, it made clear that the laws were "to be the foundation of the government . . . not to be altered by the legislative authority" under any circumstances. The charter assured broad religious freedom and trial by jury as a solid foundation for personal freedom, a promise that attracted immigrants choosing a home in the New World.

Soon after, in 1682, Penn's Frame of Government for Pennsylvania spelled out rights that were to last "for ever."

The first part of Penn's document set up the machinery of government and the powers of its various elements. The second part was what we could call a bill of rights. They included, for the first time, a ban on excessive fines, a guarantee of indictment by grand jury in capital cases, delivery to the accused of a copy of the charges against him, and assurance that a jury's verdict of not guilty was final.

Such guarantees of judicial procedure were a great departure from the arbitrary way religious and political minorities had been victimized in the past. William Penn and his fellow Quakers had suffered gross injustice in Stuart England; now in writing the Frame of Government for the new colony, Penn wanted to leave himself and later governors "no power of doing mischief, that the will of one man may not hinder the good of a whole country."

The frame also provided for the way to amend itself, the first time this essential feature of any modern constitution was written into such a document.

Returning to England for a while, Penn came back to his colony in 1699. Now he saw that the people wanted to make some political changes. Never a rigid man, he was open to new ideas. He did not think the Frame of Government was perfect and unalterable just because he had drafted it. "Friends," he once said, "if in the Constitution by charter there is anything that jars, alter it." The colonial legislature repealed the entire charter by the necessary vote in 1701, and drew up in its place a Charter of Privileges.

It was still Penn's chief concern that the colonists lose none of their liberties. The new charter safeguarded individual rights, but this time placed freedom of religion first—the prime place it would be given in the First Amendment of the federal Bill of Rights. Another protection provided was the right of counsel, something English law would not guarantee until the nineteenth century. This provision later was incorporated into the Sixth Amendment of the federal Bill of Rights.

The new Pennsylvania charter was the last colonial document to lay the basis for the constitutional protection of individual rights to be produced in the revolutionary era ahead. As the eighteenth century began, the colonial phase of charter making was nearly over. The colonists had moved far in the direction of the Constitution and Bill of Rights we now live under.

A most important point to realize is that the colonial charters and statutes could be changed by order of the Crown or Parliament. This serious limitation on power led to a clash between the colonies and Britain toward the end of the colonial period. The Americans claimed to be free of Parliament's will, to be self-governing except for sharing the king with the mother country. Many scholars think that by a strict legal reading, the British view was correct, so long as the American governments remained colonies. But Americans began to differ sharply with Britain on this vital point. And through fighting a revolution, these Americans would make their view triumphant.

3

THE SPARK OF RESISTANCE

Throughout their long history the countries of Europe had fought each other for land and wealth and power. The colonies they planted in the New World could not stay free of the troubles between the home countries. The battle for world domination between Britain and France spilled over into America in 1755. Called the French and Indian War here, it ended with the British victorious and the French driven from North America.

With the war over, the British demanded additional revenues from the colonies to help pay for the war's great cost. The British also wanted to maintain the high profits built up from their control of colonial trade. The colonial leadership elite resented British attempts to limit their opportunities and increase their taxes. The ordinary colonists, many of them poor, had never liked being exploited by their own elite, and now they resented England's attempt to milk the colonies of even more revenue. Both groups, at the upper and lower levels of American society, managed to unite in their common grievances against the British.

The American colonists, when fighting side by side with the British against the French, had felt their growing strength. Some believed they need no longer depend on the British to defend them. Why couldn't they make their own decisions? It seemed wrong that British power on the other side of the Atlantic should determine their lives over here.

Ever since the English Revolution of the seventeenth century the British Parliament had taken a major role in deciding domestic and foreign policy. But was it right for Parliament to determine colonial affairs when the colonists had no voice in that Parliament?

It was that issue—the extent of Parliament's power—that became crucial. British leaders said Parliament could have no limits placed upon its power. The Americans disagreed: They would soon reject Parliament's authority over them altogether.

But remember—this was not a quarrel simply over abstract political ideas. The Americans were not above self-interest. Social forces clashed in the developing revolutionary movement, as they do in every war or revolution. The colonists were made up of every class, from the wealthy planters and merchants to the professionals, small farmers, artisans, landless workers, women, and blacks—most of them slaves. All wanted the freedom to control their own lives and fulfill their own needs. These groups were often in conflict with one another as well as with the mother country. Eventually, as money issues became mixed with political issues, a large portion of the colonists found themselves advocating basically the same demands. Nevertheless, it is important to recognize that the colonists differed in what they thought they were fighting or struggling for. Some wanted to preserve an image of an older way of life—looking backward to models of Greece and Rome—and some had visions of a radically new way of life. What rights meant to them, of course, varied greatly depending upon their own vision of America.

The turning point for everyone came in 1764–65 when Britain tried to force the Americans to pay increased taxes while still denying them a voice in Parliament. The colonials denounced taxation without representation and took joint action in protest.

From the beginning, the American Revolution was the struggle of a colonial people for independence. At the same time, it was a revolt against monarchy. But it was also potentially a civil war—not colony against colony or region against region, or even strictly class against class, for both those who supported the Revolution (the Patriots) and those who opposed it (the Loyalists) recruited their ranks from all sections of the people. The leadership of the Revolution, however, was "upper class and moderate" as the historian Richard B. Morris described it, and feared that mobs of poor people might turn against it unless a common enemy was found.

When Parliament tried to impose the Stamp Act upon the colonies, it brought the fires of protest to a new high. The Stamp Act placed a direct tax upon dozens of things—newspapers, pamphlets, broadsides, legal documents, almanacs, even a schoolboy's diploma. In Virginia the redheaded young radical Patrick Henry, a delegate from the frontier, introduced resolutions in May 1765 that claimed no one but the assembly had the right to lay taxes upon the colony. For his argument he went back 150 years to a ruling by Coke that an Act of Parliament against the Magna Carta and the natural rights of Englishmen is null and void. The Virginians adopted a Declaration of Rights and Grievances. Published widely, the Declaration ignited debate everywhere, and other colonies soon followed Virginia's lead.

A few months later nine of the colonies, meeting in a Stamp Act Congress, issued a Declaration of Rights that asserted the colonials were all entitled to the same rights as all Englishmen, that the Stamp Act was not constitutional, and that trial by jury was the basic right of every colonist.

From Virginia the spark of resistance flew to Massachusetts, where Samuel Adams and his Sons of Liberty had already been radicalizing the colony. As early as 1762 James Otis had defended the Massachusetts legislature against an arbitrary governor, and now he attacked British taxation policy. He went back to the English Bill of Rights to claim the natural liberties of Englishmen. Of course economic matters were at stake in the conflict with the mother country, but the colonial orators and pamphleteers went beyond that to defend the essential rights and liberties of the colonists.

As the revolutionary movement swept through the

colonies, leaders such as Sam Adams saw the value of one bill of rights to state the common cause for all Americans. In 1772 Adams and a committee of the Boston Town Meeting drafted a document of rights that echoed earlier claims of freedom of conscience and trial by jury, but added new ones not found in previous colonial charters, statutes, or declarations. Among the more important were the right to be protected against unreasonable searches and seizures (it would become the Fourth Amendment), the due process clause of the Fifth Amendment, and the right to be free of attempts to establish an Episcopal Church (the First Amendment prohibition against any establishment of religion).

A year later came the Boston Tea Party, when Americans dumped British tea into the harbor rather than pay the tax demanded. That dramatic act of defiance brought heavy punishment. Britain closed the port of Boston and put Massachusetts under control of British troops. The other colonies backed Boston's rebellion, but what to do next?

In September 1774, fifty-six delegates from all the colonies but Georgia met in Philadelphia for the first Continental Congress. A mixture of moderates and radicals, they agreed to shut off trade with Britain. In a Declaration of Rights adopted on October 14, they told Britain they would no longer be bound by Parliament's laws or the king's word when it infringed on their liberties.

Restating many of the rights previously declared in one form or another, the document also coupled for the first time the right to petition with the right to assemble, thus moving closer to the language of the First Amendment. It was but a short step now to the Declaration of Independence.

As British governors were forced from power, civil authority was left vacant. A new legal basis to carry on government had to be shaped. In May 1776, the Second Continental Congress called on the colonies to suppress royal authority and set up governments of their own. That resolution was carried out; each colony drew up its own constitution to establish a new government.

By the time victory was won in the Revolutionary War, all the states had adopted written constitutions. Individual rights were firmly rooted in them. Rights were guaranteed, they held the status of supreme law, and they could be enforced against any authority that tried to defy or ignore them.

4

TREADING ON
ENCHANTED GROUND

And now, in 1776, America stood at the threshold of
its great revolution. This final quarter of the eighteenth century was "unquestionably," in the view of
the historian Michael Kammen, "the most brilliant
and creative era in the entire history of American
political thought." The ideas that developed about
self-government in the newborn nation will help us
understand difficult issues each generation faces in
applying the Bill of Rights.

Although the patriots were bent on fighting a revolution, they did not shunt aside decisions about the
kind of government they wanted to live under. Rather
than wait until independence would be achieved, they
began writing constitutions at once. They regarded a
constitution as a social compact that laid out the fundamental principles upon which the people agreed
and to which they pledged themselves. They knew
they were experimenting with risky matters, because
much of what they did was unprecedented.

Two kinds of liberty were high on their list of concerns. Civil liberty to them meant the freedom of people to act so long as what they did was not hurtful to others and was beneficial to the commonweal. Political liberty meant the freedom to take part in government, to vote, and to hold public office, not just as casual possibilities but as responsible commitments requiring wide participation if republican government was to work well. (It should be remembered—here and in what follows—that liberties and rights, as pointed out in chapter 2, were at this time restricted to certain classes of people. It took time and strife for those limits to be lifted.)

The colonists' experiences in the seventeenth and eighteenth centuries had done much to prepare them for devising the rules by which they would be governed. They had learned the need for a constitution to be a written frame of government setting fixed limits on the use of power. They rejected the old English concept that authority descends from the Crown to its officials. Theirs was the new belief that authority is derived only from the consent of the governed.

Virginia was the first state to draw up a permanent constitution, with a declaration of rights as an integral part. The legal scholar Bernard Schwartz calls it "the first true Bill of Rights in the modern American sense, since it is the first protection for the rights of the individual to be contained in a Constitution adopted by the people acting through an elected convention." It was George Mason, an almost uneducated planter with little legal training, who wrote the Virginia Declaration of Rights. He sat himself down in a tavern and without documents or books to refer to came up with the draft the convention adopted in June 1776. He was able to do this with very few changes made because of the consensus reached by Americans on the fundamental rights the law should protect.

The Virginia declaration contained many constitutional "firsts." It began with the statement that all men are created equally free and independent, with certain inherent rights, "namely, the enjoyment of life and liberty, with the means of acquiring and possessing property, and pursuing and obtaining happiness and safety." That concept—"all men are equally free"—aroused hot debate in the convention. Those who wanted it dropped said that since slavery was a part of their society, this statement of freedom and equality could ignite a slave revolt some day. The defenders of the phrase answered that slaves were not "constituent members" of their society and so the statement could not apply to blacks. The words stayed in. (Mason, like Washington and Jefferson, detested slavery, and only two years before had made a public plea for abolishing "such a wicked, cruel, and unnatural trade.")

The Virginia declaration stated that all power derives from the people, who have a right to change the government if it fails to secure its objectives. The declaration guaranteed freedom of religion and of the press. While it included clauses that anticipated the Fourth through the Eighth amendments in the federal Bill of Rights, it omitted other rights such as freedom of speech, assembly, and petition. Still, the

Virginia declaration widened the embrace of personal rights beyond what any other document before it had done. As George Mason said soon after, "Taking a retrospective view of what is passed, we seem to have been treading on enchanted ground."

While Virginia was writing her bill of rights and constitution, the Continental Congress was meeting in Philadelphia. On June 7 a Virginia delegate introduced an independence resolution in Congress. After debating it several days, the delegates set Thomas Jefferson to work on a draft of a Declaration of Independence. His manifesto, adopted on July 4, 1776, indicted England for her misdeeds, listing basic rights the Crown had invaded, and proclaiming the ties with England broken.

One of the changes Congress made in Jefferson's draft centered on the slavery issue. He had declared it a self-evident truth that "all men are created equal," and had attacked the slave trade, blaming King George for it. That section was removed upon the insistence of South Carolina and Georgia, who wished to continue the trade. Northerners too felt "a little tender" on this issue, for "though their people had very few slaves themselves," said Jefferson later, "yet they had been pretty considerable carriers of them to others."

Jefferson's declaration was not, however, a bill of rights, for it did not set forth any legal guarantees of personal freedom. Yet it was a crucial step in developments that would lead to a federal bill of rights. By breaking totally with England, the colonies created the legal authority to draw up their own constitutions and bills of rights. (Virginia had done it even before the formal Declaration of Independence.)

The other states soon followed Virginia. Seven states plus Vermont (not recognized as a state by Congress until 1791) adopted constitutions with bills of rights, and four others wrote constitutions without separate bills of rights, but with provisions in their texts assuring individual rights.

Pennsylvania (1776) was the first to follow Virginia. Her declaration of rights was very like Virginia's except that the right to counsel and the right to bear arms were added. And for the first time freedom of speech, as well as of the press, was included. Although New Jersey (1776) wrote no separate bill of rights, her new constitution banned an established church, the first such prohibition in any American constitution. (This came almost a decade before Jefferson's famous Bill for Establishing Religious Freedom was adopted in Virginia.)

Delaware (1776) put into her constitution prohibitions against housing soldiers in private homes without the owner's permission as well as laws that made certain acts illegal after the acts were committed. The most significant innovation in Maryland's declaration (1776) was a ban on bills of attainder—that is, that no person should have his rights taken away without a judicial trial. This was the forerunner of such a clause in Article I of the federal Constitution. North Carolina (1776) was the first state to insert in her declaration an implied guarantee of the right to an indictment—the direct precursor of the guarantee in the Fifth Amendment.

Both Georgia (1777) and New York (1777) placed their bills of rights within their constitutions and contributed nothing new to rights contained in other such documents. But their action underscored how common the American belief in basic rights the fundamental law must protect had become.

Vermont's constitution (1777) was the first to come from a state that had not been a separate colony before independence. All the rights it specified repeated what Virginia and Pennsylvania had set down— except, that is, for a major new provision in Article I that outlawed slavery and indentured servitude. This took the general statement about the freedom and equality of men to mean what it said. Vermont was way ahead of everyone else in this, for the federal Constitution would have nothing like it until the Thirteenth Amendment, abolishing slavery, was adopted in 1865.

South Carolina's constitution (1778) added no specific bill of rights but contained within it most of the rights commonly agreed upon. While Massachusetts had been one of the leaders in the revolt against Britain, it was one of the last states to set up a new government and adopt a constitution. The legislature itself framed a constitution in 1778, but the people rejected it overwhelmingly because it lacked a bill of rights. Responding to popular demand, it was the first state to hold a special election for a constitutional convention whose sole job was to write the document for the citizens to approve. Out of that convention came a state constitution and bill of rights (1780) written chiefly by John Adams.

5
LIBERTY WON:
HOW PRESERVE IT?

With the approval of the New Hampshire Bill of Rights in 1783, the first stage of the American struggle for written guarantees of the rights of citizens was completed. Each state ruled itself at this time, and recognized no legal authority beyond its own borders.

This was true even though the states all operated under the Articles of Confederation. That rickety frame of government had been drawn up by the Continental Congress in 1776, but was not ratified until nearly the end of the war in 1781. The only central government the former colonies had was pitifully weak and inadequate. The powers of the Congress were extremely limited. The states, jealous and uncooperative, tended to act like thirteen sovereign nations. They refused to put their trust in any central authority for fear that a few large states might dominate the rest. They quarreled among themselves over boundary lines, over court decisions, over tariffs. The war had disrupted the economy, shot living costs sky high, and plunged farmers deeply into debt. The money system was in shambles, and the grievously overburdened farmers began to take matters into their own hands.

In western Massachusetts civil war broke out when poor farmers rose up in arms. Home from fighting the Revolutionary War, they found themselves deep in debt, penniless because Congress had no funds to pay the wages owed them and the states had failed to make good their obligation. The Massachusetts veterans feared the courts would foreclose on their farms and send them off to debtors' prison. To prevent that, in 1786 about 1,500 men, led by the destitute farmer Captain Daniel Shays, descended with pitchforks on the courts and kept the judges from sitting. The frightened judges promised not to act until the farmers' grievances had been settled.

Shays's Rebellion terrified the upper classes. They feared it was the opening of a war of poor against rich, the beginning of a new revolution that would bring on frightful disorder. If the rebel movement spread, what power could put it down? The Congress could send no army against the farmers because it had no funds to pay troops.

The immediate danger passed when the governor of Massachusetts ordered 4,000 state militia out to prevent Shays's attack upon the U.S. arsenal at Springfield. The rebels were scattered, four of them killed, in a brief skirmish in January 1787. The uprising was over.

Congress was helpless in such a crisis. It sometimes could not even get a quorum to conduct business. It could not enforce the laws it passed. If it tried to amend the Articles by the required unanimous consent, it found a single state could block the move. What kind of government was it that could not get its laws obeyed, could not repay its debts, could not guarantee to meet the terms of its treaties? The wiser heads saw that only a national government that could execute its laws independently of the states could survive.

Something had to be done and done quickly, or the new nation would fall apart. Chaos could lead to tyranny. The states agreed to meet in national convention in Philadelphia to devise ways to strengthen the government so it could better meet the needs of the nation.

On May 25, 1787, fifty-five delegates from all the states but Rhode Island met, with George Washington presiding. Most of the nation's leading statesmen were there, except for Thomas Jefferson who was on duty in Paris, John Adams who was in London, and John Jay who was busy with foreign affairs.

Philadelphia was then the largest city in America. But there was nothing grand about it. Life for the average Philadelphian was, in Thomas Hobbes's phrase about the general human condition, "solitary, poor, nasty, brutish, and short." Garbage and sewage fouled streets crowded with sailors, frontiersmen, and Indians. Drunks and prostitutes hung around the waterfront taverns. But the rich lived in elegance.

With five percent of the citizens owning half of the city's taxable wealth, local government could hardly be democratic. A closed political circle of upper-class whites chose their own replacements as vacancies occurred. True, the Founding Fathers said all men are created equal, but they meant Protestant white men who owned a piece of property. (It would take another century and a half for Americans to redefine "man" to mean anybody human.)

The Constitutional Convention lasted four months, but most of its crucial decisions were made early on. The delegates immediately agreed on dropping, rather than amending, the Articles, and on writing a new Constitution. They decided to create a national government that would be supreme, and would have three branches: the legislative, the executive, and the judiciary.

It was a radical change. The articles had failed because there was no way provided to force the states to fulfill their obligations or to obey the decisions Congress made. The framers of the Constitution agreed on a government that would operate directly on individuals without the involvement of the states.

Who were the framers? Certainly not idealists playing with utopian blueprints. They were planters, lawyers, soldiers, governors, merchants, legislators. They knew the ways of the world, the mixture of good and evil in humankind. They were not novices as political leaders. Many were college trained and most had practiced law or studied it. They themselves had contended for power and wealth, and had observed the violent passions aroused in that game. They knew that power expands when there is no equal power to control it. Theirs was an unsparing view of human nature.

Experience had taught them that human beings cannot be tailored to fit some ideal system of government. Yet they did believe that the ultimate power of government resides in the people. The citizens by majority must make the laws they are to live by, and choose the officials who are to administer those laws.

Most important: Since they considered it human nature to act on self-interest, they felt that government must be strong enough to curb any tendency to greed and corruption. They also knew that when government is too powerful, it threatens liberty, so limits must be set upon governmental authority.

Inevitably there were differences among the delegates—by region, by state, by class, by personality. What they all wanted, however, was self-government, and a written constitution to make their newborn government legitimate. The lessons they had learned in writing their own state constitutions, and in observing the problem-solving experiences of the states as colonies, they brought to bear upon the drafting of the federal Constitution. But so too did they refer often to their wide reading in the literature of political thinkers.

The delegates came to Philadelphia convinced that republicanism in the form of representative government was the only conceivable political system for the United States. They had won political liberty in the war; now the great issue was how best to preserve it. By 1787 most agreed that the establishment of authority through an energetic and stable government was vital. While many of the framers hoped Americans would be virtuous, they preferred to be realistic. They looked to institutional checks rather than personal goodness as the soundest basis for maintaining liberty. Hence the need for effective separation of powers, and for a viable system of checks and balances as the structure for the new national government.

In thinking about how to improve government, political leaders divided roughly into two groups. The Federalists wanted a national government with great energy, stability, and efficiency. They feared anarchy might grow in a nation stretched over so huge a territory. Stronger and tighter control was best suited to meet the problem, they believed.

The Antifederalists worried about "unrestrained power," about placing too much power in a federal judiciary, about the "tendency to aristocracy," about insufficient separation of powers. They feared a national government that might not respond to the needs of a people so varied and scattered as the Americans.

It was the differences between large and small states and between North and South that proved more serious than any other. Whatever their differences, both the Federalists and the Antifederalists shared common ground. Both sides were committed to the republican form of government and to the protection of personal liberty. Both knew from experience that interests of various kinds—economic, social, regional—would play a big role in public affairs. And people with such conflicting interests would do their best to sway public opinion to their point of view. Yet both hoped that the art of politics would obtain harmony among the diverse groups making up the new nation. It was George Washington who, by his very presence and known support for the Federalists, did the most to make consensus possible.

Believing in liberty as all proclaimed they did, both the Federalists and the Antifederalists found the issue of slavery in a freedom-loving society deeply disturbing. Slavery and the international slave trade came up often in the secret sessions of the Constitutional Convention, though nothing was said publicly about it. Not until James Madison's detailed notes on the convention debates were published in 1840 did the public find out about the bargains made to placate South Carolina and Georgia. "The Constitution essentially protected slavery where it existed," writes the historian Michael Kammen, "and remained mute about the legality of slavery in territories that might one day become additional states. Accommodation had prevailed in 1787, as it turned out, postponing for seventy-four years the moral and political crisis of the Union."

Many delegates (even from the South) were unhappy about the taint of slavery in the Constitution. But Southern votes needed for ratification required recognition of slavery. It was a terrible price to pay for union; but if it had not been paid, the Constitutional Convention would have been wrecked. What could be more painfully embarrassing to Americans who bragged of their freedom than to be obliged to give special accommodation to slavery in the Constitution? (The word is not mentioned in the document.)

The framers knew they were not perfect nor could the Constitution be perfect. To make mistaken judgments was only human; correcting those mistakes should be made possible. As students of history they foresaw that America would grow and that the people's needs would change. So they wanted the Constitution to be open to amendment. But most of the delegates did not believe that the fundamental law they had written into the Constitution should be repealed or revised too easily or casually. They therefore made the process of changing or adding to the basic document both complex and lengthy. For an amendment to be adopted it has to win the votes of two thirds of both houses of Congress and then the votes of three fourths of the state legislatures. (The ten amendments that are the Bill of Rights would be the first to undergo this trial.)

Two thirds and three fourths are more than a simple majority. The Constitution thus closed the door on the popular majority we so often celebrate. If masses of people are swept by the passions of the moment to make a change in the Constitution, they will find it terribly hard to do. One quarter of the states, plus one, can always veto the affirmed choice of three quarters of the states minus one. If the states saying no are thinly populated, perhaps a tenth of the citizens can block the will of the remaining nine tenths. Is that good or bad? Note that in the two centuries since the adoption of the Constitution, more than 5,000 bills proposing amendments have been introduced; only twenty-six have ultimately been adopted.

By September 1787 the convention was wrapping

up its work. Yet nothing had been said about a bill of rights. Strange, for before the delegates assembled most of the states had adopted such bills. Not until September 12—only five days before it would adjourn—was a motion made to appoint a committee to prepare a bill of rights. The moment came when George Mason spoke during a debate on trial by jury. Mason, the author of the Virginia Declaration of Rights, said he wished the plan for the Constitution had been prefaced with a bill of rights, and that he would second a motion for that purpose. Mason said it would take only a few hours to draft a bill because the delegates had the state bills of rights to use as models. That fact indicates how much consensus there was on the basic rights a constitution should incorporate. Elbridge Gerry made the motion, but it was defeated unanimously (the states voting as units).

Why was Mason's proposal so quickly rejected?

It's hard to say. No delegate opposed it in principle. Perhaps one reason was the delegates' impatience to go home after sweltering for four months in Philadelphia's hottest summer on record. They may have resented the introduction of a weighty new proposal so close to the end. Only one delegate, Roger Sherman, spoke up on the proposal. He voiced the view that would soon be used to justify the omission of a bill of rights. A federal bill isn't needed, he said, because the state bills will protect the rights of their citizens. And the new federal government, he added, has not been given any power to interfere with the rights thus protected.

So the convention ended its business without drafting a bill of rights. However, the Constitution did contain some provisions protecting individual liberties which a bill of rights would normally include. Among these are the guarantees of habeas corpus (which is an order in writing issued by a judge inquiring into the lawfulness of holding a person in custody), trial by jury in criminal cases, the privileges and immunities of state citizens, and bans on bills of attainder, ex post facto laws, and religious tests.

When agreement was reached clause by clause on the basic charter of government, a committee took over to polish the draft. Gouverneur Morris was largely responsible for the wording as we know it. The Preamble, especially, is language many Americans know by heart:

> WE THE PEOPLE of the United States, in Order to form a more perfect Union, establish Justice, insure domestic Tranquility, provide for the common defence, promote the general Welfare, and secure the Blessings of Liberty to ourselves and our Posterity, DO ordain and establish this Constitution for the United States of America.

On the final day of the convention, September 17, 1787, "by unanimous consent of the States present," the Constitution was adopted and signed by thirty-nine of the delegates present. Their signatures did not mean they approved everything in the document. There were several parts that delegates took exception to. But Benjamin Franklin, the oldest delegate present, in a calm appeal to reason, said he had learned how wrong he could be in his judgments.

Drafted by men who, though wise, also had their prejudices, passions, mistaken opinions, local interests, and selfish views, this Constitution, he felt, was nevertheless astonishingly close to perfection. He could not expect a better one to come from any group, and he urged the delegates to return home and campaign ardently for its ratification.

Franklin's words, reprinted in more than fifty newspapers, would exert the most decisive influence during the heated debates in the states over ratification. Nine of the thirteen states had to approve the Constitution for it to go into effect.

It was a hard struggle to win ratification. Politicians whose careers were centered in their states would resist the loss of any power. Many people whose horizons were bounded by their home territory feared a federal government would swallow them up. Believers in the principles of liberty were dismayed to find no bill of rights in the Constitution. Others asked how come the convention had overreached itself? It was supposed to recommend only amendments to the Articles, and here it was proposing an entirely new government!

Not only that: The convention ignored the Congress in setting up the ratification process. It took the radical step of declaring ratification by nine states would be enough to create the new government. "WE THE PEOPLE" would determine the issue. Nevertheless, the Congress still voted unanimously to submit the Constitution "to a convention of delegates chosen in each state by the people thereof."

Since the delegates had met in secret session, the

public knew nothing of what had gone on. Two days after adjournment the *Pennsylvania Packet* published the Constitution, giving the entire issue to the text. Newspapers everywhere followed suit. It was the largest press any political story had received until then.

With copies of the Constitution before them, the people began a great political debate. Antifederalists opposed it, Federalists backed it. The ratifying conventions in each state revealed that the people were far from agreement on the merits of the new charter. Each faction flooded the public with articles, pamphlets, speeches, and letters, arguing their views. The strongest division between the supporters and opponents of the Constitution was the position taken over a bill of rights. The Antifederalists were deeply worried about the threat to personal liberty by a powerful central authority. They asked for many other changes in the Constitution, but focused their heaviest fire on the absence of any safeguards for civil liberties.

The Federalist defense at first was to assert that a bill of rights was not needed, since the Constitution did not give the federal government any power over individual rights and liberties, and the states had their own bills of rights. But as popular pressure mounted, they conceded the need for amendments to protect basic rights. That shifted the ground of the debate. Now the question was, should rights amendments be adopted as a condition of ratification? Or should the Constitution be ratified as it stood but with the pledge that a bill of rights would be added shortly?

Delaware was the first state to ratify the Constitution, by unanimous vote, in December 1787. One after another the states came in, but often after a strong contest with the outcome in doubt till the last ballot. It's hard to believe—after 200 years of living under the Constitution—that a switch of two, three, or ten votes by delegates in some important states would have defeated the Constitution. Only the promise of a bill of rights finally settled the outcome.

On June 21, 1788, New Hampshire ratified, providing the ninth state needed to put the Constitution into effect. The two largest states, Virginia and New York, came in later that summer, with North Carolina and Rhode Island failing to ratify until the first Congress was convened and George Washington inaugurated as president.

Though it is Washington who is acclaimed the father of his country, it is James Madison who should be recognized as the father of the Constitution. His imprint is on the Constitution more than anyone else's. Born in Montpelier, Virginia, in 1751, he helped draft his state's constitution and served in the Continental Congress. Although a small man with a weak speaking voice and a modest manner, all reports indicate he dominated the proceedings in Philadelphia. A Federalist, he arrived at the convention having thought out more thoroughly than other delegates the main problem: how to shape a strong and effective government while protecting the interests of the states and ensuring that federal power would not be abused. His Virginia Plan became the first document to circulate among the delegates, and its main features—separation of powers among the branches of government and a system of checks and balances—were adopted in the end. The most detailed records of the debates came from his pen, and his voice often prevailed at critical times in the convention.

It would be Madison again who would be chiefly responsible for the first ten amendments of the Constitution—our Bill of Rights.

6

WHAT THE PEOPLE
ARE ENTITLED TO

The first Congress under the new Constitution met
in New York in April 1789. James Madison took leadership in meeting the national demand for a bill of
rights. It was a difficult task, for the Congress was
flooded with proposals from the states for amendments, not all of them to guarantee civil liberties.
Some called for limiting federal power in general. A
few were anti–civil liberties. By one count 211 amendments had been sent in. How would he find common
ground for action?

Madison himself, it should be noted, had originally
been lukewarm about the addition of a bill of rights
to the Constitution. In a letter to his friend Jefferson
in Paris (October 17, 1788) he had said he did not
think the omission was a serious defect, yet since so
many desired a bill of rights, he favored it provided
it were done right. He called the states' bills of rights
only "parchment barriers" repeatedly violated by
"overbearing majorities." In times of popular hysteria

constitutional protection of rights was too often swept aside; the rights of the few were frequently sacrificed to the demands of the many.

But Jefferson's response and the political realities got Madison to modify his view. The ratification struggle proved that without the promise of a bill of rights the Constitution would have been defeated. When he ran for a seat in the first Congress, Madison came out in favor of amendments to assure all essential rights. After his election he acted at once to make good on his campaign promise.

Madison and Jefferson's correspondence was very influential in shaping each other's thinking. When the letters were published, the impact on many others was considerable. In one letter Jefferson writes that he approves of the Constitution generally, but goes on: "I will add what I do not like . . . the omission of a bill of rights. . . . A bill of rights is what the people are entitled to against every government on earth, general or particular, and what no just government should refuse or rest on inference." Later, commenting on Madison's assertion that a bill of rights would not be effective, Jefferson said that this was not true, "because of the legal check which [a bill of rights] puts into the hands of the judiciary."

Early in its first session the Congress was too busy with economic issues to consider other matters. Perhaps worried that the newspapers were telling the people Congress was discussing import duties while ignoring civil liberties, Madison informed the House on May 4 that he would soon introduce the subject of constitutional amendments. On June 8 he rose to

move that the House take up the matter. A congressman from Georgia told him not to be in such a hurry
to amend the Constitution. Other opponents of the
motion said there were "much more important concerns" than this, and "the discussion would take up
more time than the House could now spare." To convince them otherwise, Madison then gave one of the
great speeches in American history, explaining the
amendments on the rights of mankind he wanted to
propose, and why they were necessary.

He argued that the Congress couldn't let its first
session pass without quieting the fears of many Americans that the Constitution did not adequately protect
liberty. The great mass of the people who opposed
ratification of the Constitution did so because it lacked
a federal bill of rights. Congress had everything to
gain and nothing to lose by providing the people with
a federal bill. He then read his first draft of the crucial
amendments. It covered all the articles eventually included in the Bill of Rights and in much the same
language. And he did it by avoiding controversial provisions that might have destroyed the consensus he
was seeking. He kept in mind that he needed to win
the approval of two thirds of the House and the Senate, and three fourths of the state legislatures. The
draft shows he meant to work these rights into the
body of the Constitution.

Madison based his draft upon amendments rec-
ommended by the states, especially those of his own
Virginia. He chose them out of the huge stack sent
in, and made wise decisions, as history has proved.
Only four of his amendments were cut out during the

debate. It was Madison who dropped the flabby "ought" and "ought not" for the much stronger "shall" and "shall not." He knew the difference between effective and ineffective words. His language made the Bill of Rights "mandatory imperative," in the phrase loved by lawyers.

The "most valuable" amendment Madison wanted in the Bill of Rights was among the four rejected (by the Senate, not the House). It would have barred state violations of freedom of conscience, speech, the press, and trial by jury in criminal cases. With state power not limited in this regard, people had to rely on their particular state constitution or state bill of rights. It took the mass violence of the Civil War for significant limitations on state power's ability to infringe upon individual liberties to become part of the federal Constitution through postwar amendments.

Six weeks after his speech, the House sent Madison's amendments to a select committee, made up of one member from each state, for consideration. A week later the committee produced a report that made no basic changes in Madison's draft, except for some stylistic points. On August 13 the House began to deal with the proposed amendments, taking up freedom of religion first, and then speech, press, assembly, and petition, all to be finally embraced in the First Amendment.

One issue that came up was the meaning of sovereignty. If sovereignty rested ultimately in the people, then couldn't they always tell their representatives in government what to do? So how could a bill of rights restrict the people's desire to do whatever they wished? Madison replied: "My idea of sovereignty is, that the people can change the constitution if they please; but while the constitution exists, they must conform themselves to its dictates."

Earlier in the debate, Roger Sherman of Connecticut had urged that the amendments be adopted as a supplement at the end of the Constitution. His motion, defeated then, was adopted on August 19. "This change," says the legal historian Bernard Schwartz, "was of the greatest consequence, for it may be doubted that the Bill of Rights itself could have attained its position as the vital center of our constitutional law, if its provisions were diluted throughout the Constitution."

After a few more days of debate, the House sent the amendments to a three-man committee for proper arrangement. On August 24 the seventeen amendments they reported were agreed to by the House, and sent to the Senate for concurrence.

Unhappily, the Senate policy was for senators to meet behind closed doors. (Not until 1794 did it agree to make its sessions public.) So there is no report of the Senate debate on the Bill of Rights. Historians can go only by the skimpy reports in the Senate *Journal* and the *Annals of Congress*. Again, it would appear that the Senate was much less concerned about the Bill of Rights than were the American people. Aside from some editing and rewriting of the House version, it dropped Madison's "most valuable" amendment mentioned above. In addition it combined the two amendments concerning freedom of religion, and of

speech, press, assembly, and petition into what became the First Amendment. Closing its debate, the
Senate reduced the seventeen amendments to twelve.
On September 9 it concurred with the resolution of
the House, and then three members of the House
(Madison included) and three of the Senate met in
conference.

The conference committee made only one important change in the amendments, and it was written by
Madison. He strengthened the first guarantee of the
First Amendment in such a way that later interpretations could read it as providing for absolute separation of church and state and for the total exclusion
of government aid to religion. By September 25 both
House and Senate had agreed on the Conference report. That day they asked President Washington to
forward copies of the amendments to the states for
ratification.

We know very little about what debates took place
in the state legislatures on the proposed amendments.
At that time the states issued no official reports on
their daily proceedings. Strangely, even the newspapers had almost nothing to say about the ratification
debates. This was not because ratification was such a
sure thing that there was no excitement. In Virginia,
for instance, it took from October 1789 to December
1791 for ratification to be won. And five of the thirteen states never ratified the first two of the twelve
amendments proposed by Congress. The two amendments that did not win approval had to do with
congressional regulation of the demographic bases for

representation, and a ban on members of Congress voting to change their own salaries. Neither dealt with personal rights.

Maryland was the first state to ratify, and Virginia the last. Three states that took no official action at the time (Connecticut, Georgia, and Massachusetts) finally got around to ratification—in 1939! Their vote, of course, was not essential, for the necessary three fourths of the states had ratified by December 1791.

Now America had its Bill of Rights.

It was not handed to the people as a gift. They asked for it, they demanded it, they insisted upon it. It was their voice the Federalists were forced to listen to in their struggle to secure ratification of the Constitution. The textbooks often say the Founding Fathers wrote the Constitution. But it was the common people in the villages and towns, in the streets and in the fields, to whom we owe the Bill of Rights.

Look at the basic document as a whole, and you see the balance it strikes between the desire of the rich and the powerful to set up a strong central government to protect property rights, and the people's desire to protect human rights.

7

THE TEN AMENDMENTS

Exactly what is in the Bill of Rights?

Here is the text of each of the ten amendments, together with an explanation of its meaning:

*

AMENDMENT I
FREEDOM OF RELIGION, SPEECH, PRESS, ASSEMBLY, AND PETITION

Congress shall make no law respecting an establishment of religion, or prohibiting the free exercise thereof; or abridging the freedom of speech, or of the press; or the right of the people peaceably to assemble, and to petition the government for a redress of grievances.

The First Amendment protects five basic rights: freedom of religion, of speech, of the press, of assembly, and of petition. As with all civil liberties, these are not absolute. They must be exercised in a manner that does not conflict with the rights of others.

Congress cannot set up an official religion or place restrictions on religious beliefs. Government and religion are to be kept separate.

Freedom of speech and of the press guarantees to all people the right to express themselves freely, whether in speech or writing. The government may not censor or review books and newspapers before they are printed. The rights to assemble—to hold public meetings or demonstrations—and to petition guarantee the means to dissent or protest. The people have the right to ask the government to correct wrongs or injustices.

*

AMENDMENT II
RIGHT TO BEAR ARMS

A well-regulated militia, being necessary to the security of a free state, the right of the people to keep and bear arms, shall not be infringed.

State militia or National Guard have the right to bear arms or keep weapons. But that right is not free from government restriction. The federal government and the states can and do regulate the presence and use of firearms, such as requiring the licensing of guns and prohibiting the carrying of concealed weapons.

AMENDMENT III
LODGING TROOPS IN PRIVATE HOMES

No soldier shall, in time of peace, be quartered in any house, without the consent of the owner; nor in time of war, but in a manner to be prescribed by law.

This amendment was intended to prevent a practice like the common British one during colonial times of housing soldiers in private homes without the permission of the owners. During wartime, however, the Congress could authorize the use of private homes to house soldiers.

*

AMENDMENT IV
SEARCH AND SEIZURE

The right of the people to be secure in their persons, houses, papers, and effects against unreasonable searches and seizures, shall not be violated, and no warrants shall issue but upon probable cause, supported by oath or affirmation, and particularly describing the place to be searched, and the persons or things to be seized.

This amendment prohibits unreasonable searches and seizures. These are of two kinds: those made without warrants when warrants are required, and those that do not comply with the elements of the warrant. A proper warrant must be issued by the court (judge) and only if there is probable cause. That means an officer must convince a judge that it is likely that the search will produce evidence of a crime. A search warrant must name the exact place to be searched and the person or things to be seized. Evidence found during an unlawful search cannot be used in court.

*

AMENDMENT V
RIGHTS OF THE ACCUSED

No person shall be held to answer for a capital, or otherwise infamous, crime, unless on a presentment or indictment of a grand jury, except in cases arising in the land or naval forces, or in the militia, when in actual service in time of war or public danger; nor shall any person be subject for the same offense to be twice put in jeopardy of life and limb; nor shall be compelled, in any criminal case, to be a witness against himself; nor be deprived of life, liberty, or property, without due process of law; nor shall private property be taken for public use without just compensation.

The Fifth Amendment protects the legal rights of people in criminal proceedings. Capital crimes mean those which can be punished by death; infamous crimes are those which can be punished with prison or loss of rights. No person can be brought to trial for a felony without first being charged with a specific crime by a grand jury. A grand jury panel of twelve to twenty-three citizens must decide if the government has enough evidence to justify a trial. This procedure is meant to prevent the government from prosecuting people when it has little or no evidence of guilt. The armed forces and the militia in wartime are not covered by this rule.

No person may be tried for the same crime twice. But if a court sets aside conviction because of a legal error, the accused can be tried again. And if a person commits a crime that violates separate laws—for example, both federal and state laws—that person can be tried for that crime under each of those laws—for example, in both federal and state courts.

People may not be forced to give testimony or evidence against themselves, whether in court or in legislative inquiries. However, the prohibition against self-incrimination does not bar voluntary testimony against one's self.

A person accused of a crime is entitled to due process of law—that is, a fair hearing or trial. "Due process" refers to both the "how" and the "what" of government action. There are two forms of it—procedural and substantive. In procedural due process the government must act fairly in dealing with people. In substantive due process, it must proceed under fair laws in its relations with people.

Finally, government cannot seize private property for public use without paying the owner a fair market price for it.

AMENDMENT VI
CRIMINAL PROCEEDINGS

In all criminal prosecutions, the accused shall enjoy the right to a speedy and public trial, by an impartial jury of the state and district wherein the crime shall have been committed, which district shall have been previously ascertained by law, and to be informed of the nature and cause of the accusation; to be confronted with the witnesses against him; to have compulsory process for obtaining witnesses in his favor and to have the assistance of counsel for his defense.

This amendment protects the procedural rights of people in criminal cases. The right to a speedy and public trial is to prevent a person from being warehoused in jail indefinitely or being tried secretly by a court. But time must be allowed for preparing an adequate defense. If the government postpones trial so that it becomes hard for a person to get a fair hearing, the charge may be dropped. A trial can be moved from the district where the crime was committed if public prejudice might affect the impartiality of the trial.

Accused persons must be told the charges against them, and allowed to question witnesses for the prosecution. Witnesses who might help the accused can be ordered to appear in court, and can be held in contempt if they refuse to comply with a subpoena.

Accused persons must be allowed to have a lawyer unless they choose to act as their own counsel. The government must provide a lawyer if the accused cannot afford one. The right to counsel has been held to cover the period of police interrogation as well as trial.

AMENDMENT VII
JURY TRIAL IN CIVIL CASES

In suits at common law, where the value in controversy shall exceed twenty dollars, the right of trial by jury shall be preserved, and no fact tried by a jury shall be otherwise re-examined in any court of the United States than according to the rules of the common law.

Civil suits involve parties contesting private matters. Common law refers to rules of law established by judges in past cases. While in criminal cases the government is always the prosecutor, it may or may not be a party in a civil suit. When it is a party, it can be either the plaintiff (the party wronged) or the defendant (the party being held accountable). An appeals court cannot change a verdict because it disagrees with the jury. It can set aside a verdict only if legal errors made the trial unfair.

AMENDMENT VIII
BAIL AND PUNISHMENT

Excessive bail shall not be required, nor excessive fines imposed, nor cruel and unusual punishments inflicted.

Bail is money deposited with the court to obtain the release of the accused from jail pending trial. The court sets bail at the time of arraignment. If the accused does not appear for trial, the government keeps the money. This amendment forbids courts to set excessive, or unreasonably high, bail. The amount of bail usually depends on the seriousness of the charge and whether the accused is likely to appear for the trial. A punishment must not be cruel or unusual, such as mental or physical torture.

*

AMENDMENT IX
RIGHTS RESERVED TO THE PEOPLE

The enumeration in the Constitution, of certain rights, shall not be construed to deny or disparage others retained by the people.

The Constitution does not specifically list all rights of the people. They retain certain rights that are not listed in the Constitution.

AMENDMENT X
POWERS RESERVED TO THE STATES

The powers not delegated to the United States by the Constitution, nor prohibited by it to the states, are reserved to the states respectively, or to the people.

This amendment protects the powers reserved to the states. Powers not given to the federal government belong to the states, or to the people. The amendment thus limits the power of the federal government.

The Bill of Rights did much to strengthen the democratic standard of equality proclaimed as a self-evident truth in the Declaration of Independence. Yet the lack of that "most valuable amendment" Madison had tried, and failed, to insert in the Bill of Rights (see page 53) made it possible for the states to violate the individual's rights.

The states had their own constitutions and bills of rights. While they were much like the federal rights, there were some differences. And just as importantly, each state's judges interpreted those rights differently. So a citizen in one state might have a set of civil liberties different from those of a citizen in another state.

Not until 1868—almost a hundred years after Madison's "most valuable amendment" was rejected—was this grave problem remedied when the Fourteenth Amendment was ratified. Now the Constitution explicitly gave every citizen, anywhere in the

United States, equal protection under the law.

Here is what Section I of Amendment 14 declares:

All persons born or naturalized in the United States, and subject to the jurisdiction thereof, are citizens of the United States and of the State wherein they reside. No State shall make or enforce any law which shall abridge the privileges or immunities of citizens of the United States; nor shall any State deprive any person of life, liberty, or property without due process of law; nor deny to any person within its jurisdiction the equal protection of the laws.

The Fourteenth Amendment was one of the great measures that emerged from the Civil War of 1861–65. That conflict ended in the destruction of slavery. When freedom came for all blacks, Congress and the president faced the task of making new laws that would affect not only the freed people and the defeated slaveholders but the whole nation. Three Constitutional amendments were adopted and ratified. The Thirteenth said slavery was now against the law. The Fifteenth gave black males the right to vote. The Fourteenth had these main purposes: to make national citizenship paramount to state citizenship; to confer national citizenship upon the newly freed slaves; and to secure for the former slaves the enjoyment of certain civil rights.

The Fourteenth Amendment's guarantee of "equal protection of the laws" transformed the constitutional system. For although the Bill of Rights protected citizens from certain excesses of power by the *national* government, there were no guarantees that rights would be protected by all the *states* (as the former slave states—and many places in the North as well—had shown they would not be). The Fourteenth made possible the extension of political and civil liberties to *all* persons, regardless of race, creed, status, or wealth.

If the Fourteenth had not been ratified, life for many citizens would have been very different. Blacks and members of other minority groups might still face barriers to voting, education, housing, jobs, and other privileges and immunities they are entitled to as citizens of the United States. The fruits of the Fourteenth Amendment, in the words of a Supreme Court Justice, constitute "the most profound and pervasive revolution ever achieved by substantially peaceful means."

Only gradually, however, and never completely, did the U.S. Supreme Court accept the Fourteenth Amendment as a standard that would guarantee due process and equal protection of the laws for all persons. Many judges did not agree, as we shall see.

And in the states the same slow process made change just as gradual. It has taken over a hundred years for Supreme Court decisions to bind the fifty states to accept most of the guarantees for their citizens that the federal Bill of Rights contains.

8

IF THERE IS ANY FIXED STAR

By 1791, then, the civil liberties cherished by Americans from colonial times had been made part of the fundamental law of the land. The adoption of the Bill of Rights was a great victory. But do such victories endure forever?

When citizens struggle to protect their constitutional rights in any given historical moment, whatever gains they may make do not necessarily protect citizens in the future. Each generation has to stand up for its rights—or lose them.

So the task of defending liberty goes on. Even when people we take as friends of liberty are elected to high office, we cannot sit back and assume all will be well. Thomas Jefferson himself abused the powers of the presidency when he held office. So did Abraham Lincoln. So did Franklin D. Roosevelt. It seems that people holding great power find it possible to violate the Constitution so long as they can tell themselves, "It's all right in *this* case; I know it's for the good of the country."

The Constitution was meant by the Founding Fathers to be the permanent foundation of the nation. But they knew it must evolve with time and changing circumstances. That was why they provided for a method of amending it. For the Constitution to continue to be effective, new groups entering or developing in America (like the freed slaves) had to be assured the benefits of traditional rights. New ways had to be created to solve persistent problems. Old rights had to be interpreted to enable them to meet new circumstances. Wise as the Founders were, they could not see beyond the horizon of the eighteenth century. The culture of anyone's time sets limits on the vision of all but the greatest genius.

What we'll do here is sketch some of the changes that have occurred in American life in the 200 years since 1791, and indicate how they have affected our constitutional rights. You might think there's nothing difficult about this. Don't such simple phrases as "freedom of speech" or "freedom of religion" mean what they say? Yes, but what *do* they mean? The responses to that question range widely, shaped by the history of the amendment, the temperament and upbringing of the judges, by their preferences and prejudices, their politics and passions.

Let's start with freedom of religion, the first part of the First Amendment. As presented there, it has to do with two things: separation of church and state, and the free exercise of religion. The establishment clause forbids a state or the federal government to set up a church. Neither one can pass laws to aid one religion or all religions, or to prefer one over another. People cannot be forced to go to or remain away from a church, or to profess a belief or disbelief in any religion. No one can be taxed to support any religious activity or institution.

Under the establishment clause fall the conflicts about such matters as state and federal aid to religious organizations and schools, the legality of allowing or requiring school prayer, and the teaching of evolution versus fundamentalist theories of creation.

In decisions of 1962 and 1963 the Supreme Court outlawed daily readings of the Bible and recitation of prayers in public schools. Despite these rulings, many school districts, particularly in the South, continue to violate the Court's prayer ban. Advocates of school prayer have proposed a Constitutional amendment to overturn the Court's rulings, but so far it has failed passage in the Congress.

Governmental aid to church-related private schools has been denied by the Court if it is meant to subsidize religious instruction. In a series of cases the Court has allowed states to use tax funds only if the aid is secular in aim—for lunches, textbooks, diagnostic services, standardized tests, transportation, and the like. The government, said the Court, must avoid "an excessive entanglement with religion."

But the Court does not disapprove of a recent change in attitudes toward teaching *about* religion in the public schools. For decades educators had shied away from classroom discussion of religion. It was too divisive a subject, they feared. Or it might breach separation between church and state.

Yet religion is undeniably a major force in American culture as well as in world history. How can it be ignored? Gradually, in recent years, state by state, social studies courses are being revised to include religion as a topic in both elementary and secondary schools. It is felt that, as the California Department of Education put it, "Students must become familiar with the basic ideas of the major religions and ethical foundation of each time and place."

Both conservatives and liberals believe there is a need to discuss religion in the public schools. Conservatives support the idea because they think the absence of religion carries an implicit antireligious message. Liberals believe that learning about the many different religions strengthens pluralism.

Educators don't want the public schools to promote religious beliefs or classroom prayer. They stress that Supreme Court decisions bar religious exercises in public schools while they affirm that the Constitution permits the discussion of religions as part of a far broader curriculum.

As an example of what is being tried, there is a Connecticut high school that offers a course on world religions that is so popular almost all the 1,100 students enroll in it. The course covers religion in general as a force in human affairs, and then devotes units of study to Christianity, Judaism, Islam, Hinduism, Buddhism, Zoroastrianism, Sikhism, and other beliefs.

The subject is so new and teachers so unfamiliar

with it that workshops are offered throughout the country to give teachers the background and training they need for such courses.

The other aspect of the First Amendment is the constraint it places on Congress not to prohibit the free exercise of religion. People are free to hold any or no religious belief. But if a religious *practice* works against public policy or the public welfare, the Court has held that the government may step in. It can require certain types of vaccinations, for instance, regardless of the child's or the parents' religious beliefs. Judicial decision becomes difficult and complex at times: The children of Jehovah's Witnesses are not required to say the Pledge of Allegiance at school, but their parents can't stop them from getting medical treatment (such as blood transfusions) if their lives are in danger.

America is generally seen as a country offering more religious freedom and diversity than any other nation. That developed because religious freedom is deeply rooted in the Bill of Rights. The crucial link between religious freedom and the First Amendment is often overlooked by those who call for government aid to religion. They tend to view opposition to government support of religion as opposition to religion itself. They identify their cause with God and religion, and label the opponents of government aid as atheists or secular humanists. Such charges confuse the public about the First Amendment principle of religious freedom and diversity, and threaten to divide the country along political-religious lines. The Founding

Fathers understood—from a long history of religious persecution—that church and state are best served by separation rather than fusion.

If we glance back at our early history, the reasons for placing religious freedom in the First Amendment may become clearer. The quest for that freedom was one of the motives for emigration to America, but not just for those who wanted to be free to practice their own faith. A surprising majority of colonial Americans were not part of any religious community. Even in New England, research shows, not more than one person in seven was a church member. It was one in fifteen in the middle colonies and fewer still in the South, according to the historian Richard Hofstadter.

Religious toleration developed only slowly in the colonies. In nine of the thirteen colonies religion was established by law, giving one church in the colony almost a monopoly on religious and moral practices. Under Puritan control of Massachusetts Bay Colony, people with differing religious beliefs were often fined, whipped, jailed, banished, or even executed. Roman Catholics, Jews, Anabaptists, Native Americans, and African Americans in many places were persecuted for practicing their religions. No wonder, then, that the Revolution's leaders, including Madison, Jefferson, and Washington, believed ardently in the importance of guaranteeing freedom of religion.

Later, in 1943, Justice Robert H. Jackson, in his decision sustaining the right of Jehovah's Witnesses to refrain from the flag salute, expressed beautifully the basic principle of the Founding Fathers:

If there is any fixed star in our constitutional constellation, it is that no official, high or petty, can prescribe what shall be orthodox in politics, nationalism, religion, or other matters of opinion, or force citizens to confess by word or act their faith therein.

9

THE RIGHT TO DISSENT

Perhaps no part of the First Amendment is more frequently invoked than the right to free speech and a free press. It is the very bedrock of our democratic system. For a true democracy to flourish, people must have a say in the decisions that shape their lives. Without the free flow of information and ideas, how can a citizen determine what policy to support? Or what candidate to vote for?

In a self-governing society the citizen has big responsibilities: to try to understand the issues that face the nation; to pass judgment on the decisions the legislators make on these issues; and to help figure out the best way to make these decisions effective, or, if necessary, how to replace mistaken decisions with better ones.

Public opinion ought to play a major role in the decisions of a democracy. It is out of the give and take of free speech and a free press that public opinion emerges. Without an open exchange of views the acts of legislatures and officials become arbitrary and tyrannical.

Most Americans today would say they agree on the value of and right to free expression. But was it always this way? Not at all, contrary to popular myth. To go back to the beginnings, colonial America never greeted warmly the advocates of what they considered obnoxious or detestable ideas. Narrow-minded Puritans and domineering royal judges hated anything unorthodox. And they did not stand alone. For the people too, as Professor Leonard Levy's research demonstrates, "simply did not understand that freedom of thought and expression means equal freedom for the other fellow, particularly the one with the hated ideas." Each small community in those days tended to hold tight to its own brand of orthodoxy, ready to get rid of or punish any "outsider" with unwelcome opinions.

Central to the popular myth about freedom of the press in colonial America is the story of John Peter Zenger. His trial for seditious libel of the royal governor of New York is celebrated as a great victory for freedom of the press. Zenger, a German immigrant, was the printer of the *New-York Weekly Journal*, chosen for that job by a political faction opposing Governor Cosby. Zenger, though neither the editor nor the writer, was tried for the paper's seditious libel of the governor. Zenger's lawyer pleaded truth as a defense and the jury acquitted the printer.

This was taken as a great advance for the right to publish without restraint. But the common law on criminal libel was never questioned. Zenger won the case only because his fellow colonials in the jury box agreed with the newspaper's remarks about the governor. But what if a defendant's views are unpopular? "A jury, then as today," writes Professor Levy, "was essentially a court of public opinion, often synonymous with the public prejudice. Moreover, the opinions of men notoriously differ: one man's truth is another's falsehood. Indeed political opinions may be neither true or false and are usually not capable of being proved by the rules of evidence, even if true."

Americans accepted the British or common-law definition of freedom of the press. At the time the First Amendment was adopted, people like Jefferson and Madison believed that punishment of a seditious libeler did not abridge freedom of the press.

But "seditious libel" is only another name for political dissent. Allow people to speak up freely and what they say is almost always sure to offend someone. No strongly held opinion will ever be unanimously agreed to. In time of trouble and turmoil especially, the First Amendment rights meet their toughest test. It is at such moments of crisis that curbs on expression have often been legislated. In 1798, only seven years after the Bill of Rights became part of the Constitution, the Congress passed the Alien and Sedition Acts. They were intended to prevent criticism of the government. At that time, war with France seemed very likely. The Federalists, under President John Adams, were the government in power. Because they were advised of a conspiracy against the United States, supposedly directed by foreign agents, they got the Congress to pass four restrictive laws. Three were aimed at foreigners—especially Frenchmen and Irishmen, looked on as dangerous revolutionaries. Such aliens could be deported or confined during war. Hundreds of Frenchmen, suspected of being plotters, were deported. The fourth and worst law, the Sedition Act, made it a crime punishable by fine and imprisonment to speak, write, or publish false, scandalous, and malicious statements about the president, Congress, or the government "with intent to defame" or with intent to "excite against the government the hatred of the people."

These laws plainly violated the First Amendment and aroused protests throughout the nation. Yet dozens of people were prosecuted under them and ten, all of them editors or printers supporting Jefferson, were actually put in prison for speaking or writing against government policy.

How could that be? The answer lies in the fact that the British common law of "seditious libel" still operated in America. While the government could not prevent speech or publication in advance (this is called "prior restraint"), it could legally punish the speaker or writer after the expression of critical opinions of government that tended to make people think less of it. The First Amendment did not knock down the common law. It barred censorship in advance of publication, but a person was accountable under the criminal law for abuse of the right to speak or publish freely.

Punishment *after* the fact effectively scares people off from saying what they think. It punches holes in the wall of protection the First Amendment would seem to be. In Madison's words, "It would seem a mockery to say that no laws shall be passed preventing publication from being made, but that laws might be passed for punishing them in case they should be made."

The Sedition Act was aimed at Jeffersonians who strongly opposed the policy of John Adams and the Federalists. It was their editors who were jailed under the Sedition Act. As a besieged minority the Jeffersonians struggled to maintain their party and to hang on to the right to function unfettered. The Sedition Act provoked them to develop a new approach to the issue of seditious libel. Several wrote pamphlets or books that led to the abandonment of the common-law doctrine of seditious libel. The very idea that there was such a crime was denounced. These libertarians held that a free government cannot be criminally attacked by the opinions of its citizens. They insisted that freedom of the press, like chastity, was either absolute or it did not exist. The notion of *verbal* political crimes must be scrapped, they said. Only injurious *conduct*, shown by overt acts or deeds, not words, might be subject to criminal charges.

This interpretation of the First Amendment grew out of the then-novel theory that a democracy must have freedom of political discussion or its existence and security are endangered. The very nature of a democratic government means that it is the servant of the people, not their master. It exists by their consent and for their benefit. It cannot, therefore, tell the citizens what they shall think.

The uproar caused by the Alien and Sedition Acts

ended when Adams and the Federalists were voted out of office and Jefferson entered the White House. He issued pardons to persons punished under the acts, and the acts themselves lapsed in 1801. While the Supreme Court never ruled on the Sedition Act, the Jeffersonian attacks upon its validity "carried the day in the court of history," as Justice William Brennan commented long after.

Admired as a great patriot with an ardent passion for freedom, Jefferson looms larger than life. But he was only human; he too exhibited weaknesses and sometimes acted against his own principles. In the several high offices he held, he was on the wrong side of liberty many times. Though he opposed the Alien and Sedition Acts privately, he never publicly declared his opposition during the years of hysteria. And when he was in the presidency, he didn't like the loud opposition he heard any more than Adams had. He launched federal sedition prosecutions against *his* political opponents. Acts he once condemned as shocking betrayals of constitutional rights suddenly turned innocent when the government was in his hands. As with many of us, principle and practice were not always in harmony.

Unhappily, the Alien and Sedition period was not the only time the criminal law was stretched to cover political dissent. It was but the first. After it came a long succession of laws against specific "political crimes." For legislatures have continually tried to curb political movements they disapprove of. Sometimes they write new laws, sometimes they make use of existing ones to control or oppose a demand for social change—

the antislavery movement, the labor movement, the civil rights movement, the peace movement, the environmental movement. Any and every citizen protest that some politician or power decides is "subversive" becomes a target for persecution.

There is no evidence that such actions in defiance of the First Amendment have ever had any significant value in promoting the general welfare in a democratic society. Instead, they invariably wreak havoc on the basic freedoms of our society.

We mentioned earlier that the Supreme Court did not rule on the Alien and Sedition Acts. It was not until 1803, soon after those acts lapsed, that the Court for the first time held an act of Congress unconstitutional. The details of the case—*Marbury v. Madison*—need not be gone into here; it is remembered because of the reasoning of Chief Justice John Marshall. His justification for judicial review of an act of Congress by the Supreme Court has served as a precedent ever since.

When Madison drafted the Bill of Rights, he believed that independent courts would act as the guardians of those rights. Judicial review was an implied aspect of the Constitution's design. The guarantee of the first ten amendments would be only empty words unless directly enforced by the courts. Their duty would be to declare void all acts contrary to those guarantees. That is what happened in the states during the time of the Articles of Confederation. At least eight states directly asserted the power of judicial review in various cases before their courts.

But in federal cases the crucial element of judicial

review was not spelled out until *Marbury v. Madison.*
Now the high court had the power to nullify laws that
went beyond the government's limited authority. (The
courts can also enjoin the executive branch if it violates
individual rights or exercises powers exclusively reserved for Congress.)

Is that enough to safeguard civil liberties? No, because the courts cannot move on their own. The president and Congress do not need a court's approval
before they act. And the courts cannot take action on
their own initiative to strike down unconstitutional
laws or government actions. To bring in the power of
judicial review, an individual or group must challenge
a particular government action. And such suit must
be brought by those directly harmed by the government's action. As an example, if Congress passes a
law barring citizens from handing out leaflets, any
citizen affected by that law may challenge it in court.
The court is then empowered to decide whether the
law violates the citizen's constitutional rights.

What this means is that citizen action is vital to the
assertion of constitutional rights. Number One, you
have the Bill of Rights; Number Two, you have the
independent courts; but Number Three, you must
have someone to assert those rights for the constitutionality of the law to be tested.

It was the struggle for black freedom that gave the
Bill of Rights its most severe testing throughout much
of American history. From the earliest days of the
Republic abolitionists black and white made stirring
use of the spoken and printed word to rally support
for the overthrow of slavery. And from the beginning

the harshest means were used to stifle their voices, censor their publications, wreck their presses, cripple their organizations, and jail or murder their leaders. The First Amendment freedoms of speech, of the press, of assembly, of petition were violated countless times, not only in slavery's stronghold, the South, but in the North as well.

In Georgia, just for subscribing to the antislavery paper *The Liberator*, a man was tarred, feathered, horse-whipped, and half drowned. A number of whites in the South were killed for meeting with blacks in public. In Tennessee a Bible salesman was charged with distributing abolitionist literature and whipped by a mob in the public square. In South Carolina a mob sacked the federal post office and burned all abolitionist literature awaiting delivery. The Postmaster General then excused Southern postmasters from delivering abolitionist material. Southerners in the House of Representatives got a "gag" rule passed that for five years bottled up all antislavery petitions. In the North lecturers traveling the towns to plead the cause of the slave had public halls denied them and meetings broken up.

The pressure to conform was enormous. When Lydia Maria Child, the editor of the popular *Juvenile Miscellany*, publicly declared herself against slavery, all her Southern readers canceled their subscriptions and put the children's magazine out of business. Because of her abolitionist stand, the Boston Athenaeum refused to let her use their research library. When the *Liberator*'s editor, William Lloyd Garrison, spoke to the Boston Female Antislavery Society, a mob burst in with cries of "Lynch him!" and dragged him through the streets. In the midwest the abolitionist editor Elijah Lovejoy saw three of his printing presses thrown into the river by mobs, and when he defended a fourth press, the killers shot him dead. John Greenleaf Whittier, the antislavery poet, faced down mobs at least four times. In Alabama a grand jury indicted a New Yorker for having mailed a copy of an antislavery paper into the state, and demanded that New York officials extradite him for trial.

Did the First Amendment prevent any of these outrages? Did it remedy any of the wrongs done? Never. The Bill of Rights was taken to mean "for whites only." And if any whites acted in sympathy with blacks, the Constitution no longer applied to them either. As a matter of record, after *Marbury v. Madison* the Supreme Court never decided on the constitutionality of any act until 1857, when Chief Justice Roger B. Taney handed down the infamous decision in the case of Dred Scott, a Missouri slave. Scott claimed he was free because of temporary residence on free soil. Taney held that Scott was not a citizen, that no free black had ever been one. Blacks, he went on, were "so far inferior that they had no rights which the white man was bound to respect." Going further, he ruled that the Missouri Compromise of 1820 was unconstitutional because "Congress had no power to abolish or prevent slavery in any of the territories." His words denied all hope of justice for blacks.

Southern power, massed in the federal government (Southerners controlled the Supreme Court, the House and the Senate, the presidency and the cabinet) had its way. Nearly forty years after its adoption and for the first time in U.S. history, the Missouri Compromise—a major law enacted by Congress—was struck down by the Supreme Court. Taney's Dred Scott ruling delighted the South and infuriated the North.

Reading history, one can only question whether judicial decisions are above the fray. How can they not be influenced by the judge's class, color, education, politics, prejudices? Not automatically and not always. Some judges astonish the public by their decisions. Their views of the facts and their interpretations of them in light of the Constitution may depart radically from what is expected of them by the presidents who appointed them.

10

FREEDOM— AND THE WITCH-HUNT

Every time we celebrate some anniversary of our revolutionary origins, we pay tribute to the great American tradition of freedom. But there is another American tradition that is embarrassing to bring up. It is even older than the Bill of Rights and has proved just as durable. I mean the witch-hunt. The Bill of Rights and the witch-hunt: opposites. The one we honor, the other we deplore; the one we want to preserve, the other we'd like to get rid of. Yet so long as people hold unpopular ideas, so long will they be persecuted for them.

In the last chapter we saw how savagely many Americans hounded the blacks and whites who spoke out against slavery. Freedom of speech, of press, of assembly, and of petition were denied to the advocates of emancipation. Each branch of government—the legislative, the executive, the judicial—contributed to the denial of rights to persons it considered a threat.

That pattern of combined action against dissenters

blots the pages of our history. In the twentieth century, it happened again and again, sometimes persisting for years. In 1917, when America entered the First World War, Congress passed the Espionage Act. It gave the government the power to censor the press, ban publications from the mail, and imprison anyone who interfered with the conscription or the enlistment of soldiers. It was a powerful means of silencing opposition to the war. If President Woodrow Wilson could not have loyalty freely given, he would compel it.

Many Americans believed it was wrong for the country to get involved in the conflict that had been killing millions of young men and devastating Europe since 1914. They were a minority, but a militant one. Under the Espionage Act the government suppressed many newspapers and magazines, no matter how light their criticism of any detail of the war effort. Thousands of people were jailed for talking or writing against the war. Far more were scared into hiding their views. The president helped spread the virus of fear. He attacked "hyphenated Americans"—meaning especially those of German descent—accusing them of disloyalty and anarchy. He whipped up such violent prejudice, mixed with a phobia against radical ideas, that a mob in Missouri lynched a young German-born citizen. In Chicago the government played on war hysteria to convict one hundred trade unionists of sabotage and conspiracy to obstruct the war. Over half of them got sentences of ten or twenty years in prison. Much of the American Socialist leadership was sent to prison. Academics such as Scott Nearing were fired for speaking or writing against the war. The nation's public schools were turned into propaganda agencies to make war appear a glamorous adventure, while any discussion of the causes of war, such as nationalism or imperialism, was forbidden.

Using the antialien and antiradical passions ignited by government during the war, federal agencies launched a Red Scare in 1919. Attorney General A. Mitchell Palmer (aided by a young assistant, J. Edgar Hoover) ordered a mass roundup of "Reds." On January 2, 1920, his men raided thirty-three cities and netted, mostly without warrants, more than 10,000 "suspected" radicals, most of them immigrants. The victims were held for days, weeks, months, to be deported "back to where they came from" or jailed under twenty-year sentences. "Alien filth," Attorney General Palmer called them.

In that Red Scare thousands of men and women, radical or not, who had a constitutional right to their beliefs, suffered terribly. The weak and fragmented radical movement of that time was no threat to anyone. Yet the Department of Justice, instead of protecting the Bill of Rights, swept it aside. It set a pattern of ruthless suppression that would last throughout the century.

With the close of World War II in 1945, it happened again. This time gross violations of the Bill of Rights were the product of the Cold War. The mood of the Palmer Days seized the country once more. Out of the war the Soviet Union emerged as a power rivaling the United States in strength and influence. Communist regimes took control of much of Eastern

Europe and soon of vast China. While during the war the U.S.S.R. and the U.S. had been allies, after it a dominant wing of American opinion urged anti-Communist moves in Europe and the Far East. A militant campaign began against dissent at home and abroad. Communism was said to be a great threat to our cherished freedoms and to national security. In so great a crisis, it was dangerous to permit the unchecked flow of ideas.

Traditionally this argument has been the excuse given by the powerful to suppress freedom. Yet in times of emergency, civil liberties are all the more essential. The nation needs every critical and constructive voice to help guide it through whatever danger is threatening.

The Red Scare was easily made into a political tool to help win elections. Clever campaign slogans, such as the charge by the Republicans that the Democrats stood for "Communism, Chaos and Corruption," froze voters' minds and bypassed the real issues facing the nation. When President Harry Truman began preparing in 1947 for the forthcoming presidential race, he stole the Republican thunder by launching his Loyalty Program. This was actually the beginning of what soon became called "McCarthyism."

Under Truman's plan all government workers had to pass a test of their beliefs and associations. They would be fired for membership in, affiliation with, or sympathy for "any foreign or domestic organization, association, movement, group or combination of persons designated by the Attorney General as totalitarian, Fascist, Communist or subversive." The program cast a huge net to entangle people through guilt by association.

The attorney general issued a list of "subversive" groups, to guide the Loyalty Program. He designated a long roster of organizations as subversive without notifying them or giving them a chance to refute the charge. Such administrative procedures violated constitutional assurances of due process. It did not bother the government. Millions of people were investigated by loyalty boards to see whether at some future date they might commit a disloyal act. They were asked what books and magazines they read, what plays or movies they saw, what friends they had, what groups they belonged to. Did they ever have blacks in their homes? How did they feel about poor people?

The assurances of fair trial found in the Bill of Rights were ignored. Once accused, a federal employee had to prove his or her innocence. (It was like the procedure in the Salem witch trials: We say you're a witch. Prove you're not!) No impartial judge, no jury of one's peers, no chance to confront and cross-examine accusers, no protection from double jeopardy.

No one victimized by a loyalty board was ever indicted for an illegal act. Yet thousands lost their jobs and had their lives ruined. And as always happens in time of intimidation, many thousands more learned to shut up.

One after another, city and state legislatures and the Congress passed laws against "subversives." Truman followed up his Loyalty Program with the indictment by a federal grand jury in 1948 of twelve

Communist Party leaders under the Smith Act of 1940. That law punished not only conspiracy to overthrow the government but also *advocacy* or *conspiracy to advocate* its overthrow. In other words, not the deed itself but the teaching of a political idea. This clearly limited freedom of speech, press, and association. (Under such a law Patrick Henry and Thomas Jefferson could have been sent to prison long before 1776.) The government arrested more than a hundred Communist party officials and convicted most of them. A Supreme Court majority held it was all right in their case to sacrifice free speech because the Communists were "a clear and present danger" to the nation's security.

With scores of men and women going to jail, anyone who might be linked in any way to unorthodox political beliefs and practices had great reason to fear trouble. Various legislative committees—local, state, and federal—stepped in to ferret out radicals in government, the universities, the press, radio, and the movies. The leader was the House Un-American Activities Committee (HUAC). It said bluntly that its real purpose was not to gather facts upon which to base legislation but to inform the public of subversives "by turning the light of pitiless publicity" on them. The chief function of HUAC, said its chairman, J. Parnell Thomas, "has always been the exposure of un-American individuals and their un-American activities."

Congress has the right to conduct investigations. The investigations are meant to produce facts that might help provide legislative solutions to important problems. They enable Congress to review how the tax-payers' money is spent and to keep an eye on the conduct of public officials and of special interest groups.

But the role of Congress is not to determine whether an individual is innocent or guilty of a crime. The Constitution bars that. We have the courts for that purpose. From time to time some committees have gone far beyond their legal functions, to engage in the trial of citizens. The punitive exposure of people who could not be found guilty of violating any law was their goal. HUAC and Senate committees such as Senator Joseph McCarthy's and Senator James Eastland's raised the specter of a plot to overthrow the government by force or violence. They hauled in teachers, editors, actors, writers, doctors, mechanics, scientists, labor leaders, and housewives, and grilled them on their political beliefs and associations.

When HUAC prepared for hearings, the witnesses subpoenaed were divided into two groups, "friendly" and "unfriendly." The first supported the witch-hunt and helped carry it out. The second resisted the committee's grilling.

Congress has the power to subpoena witnesses to get information from them. But the "only legitimate object" for such testimony, the Supreme Court has ruled, is to obtain pertinent information "to aid it in legislating." The rights of witnesses must be given "due regard," and witnesses "rightfully may refuse to answer when the bounds of power are exceeded," the Court has said.

Perhaps the best-known example of HUAC's violation of a citizen's right to freedom of expression is the case of the Hollywood Ten. This occurred in 1947 when at public hearings friendly witnesses supported HUAC's claim that the movie industry was riddled with Communists and its pictures filled with their propaganda. No evidence was produced to support that sweeping charge. The unfriendly witnesses—eight writers, one director, and one producer—refused to answer the question asking whether they had been members of the Communist party. They claimed the free speech guarantee of the First Amendment protects the individual from being compelled to disclose his beliefs and associations. The committee cited them for contempt—willful disobedience to the order of a court or legislative body. They were convicted at trial, and all were fired from their jobs by the movie studios. The federal Court of Appeals rejected their use of the First as a defense, and the Supreme Court refused to review the decision. They each went to prison for a year.

The Supreme Court failed to address the First Amendment issue in many of these cases. The justices turned instead to technicalities of one kind or another as the basis for their decisions.

Other witnesses before HUAC and similar bodies met the same fate as the Hollywood Ten. The committees rode high in those years of the Cold War. As Justice William Douglas put it, they could "depart with impunity from their legislative functions, sit as kangaroo courts, and try men for their loyalty and their political beliefs."

The merit of the views held by people hauled before the committees is not the issue. What is significant is their right to advocate and organize, free of government interference, for the purpose of challenging policy or proposing change. When that First Amendment right is interfered with, it is a criminal act of political repression. In the 1940s and 1950s it led to a revival of the practice of blacklisting. This is part of the dark side of the American tradition. The blacklist, which costs people their jobs, operated on the campus, in the schools, in the media, in the labor movement, in business and industry, in the scientific community, and throughout government. It is always symptomatic of the great fear of dissent which every now and then grips our society.

The cost to the victims is enormous. In 1961, after the Supreme Court ruled five to four to uphold a HUAC contempt citation, Justice Hugo Black, of the minority, spoke from the bench:

From now on anyone who takes a public position contrary to that being urged by the House Un-American Activities Committee should realize that he runs the risk of being subpoenaed to appear at a hearing in some far-off place, of being questioned with regard to every minute detail of his past life, of being asked to report all the gossip he may have heard about any of his friends and acquaintances, of being accused by the Committee of membership in the Communist Party, of being held up to the public as a subversive and traitor, of being jailed for contempt if he refuses to cooperate with the Committee in its probe of his mind and associations, and of being branded by his neighbors, employer, and erstwhile friends as a menace to society regardless of the outcome of that hearing.

McCarthyism is but another name for what HUAC had been doing many years before the senator from Wisconsin came to Washington. Yet because of his flamboyance and the wild extravagance of his charges, his name dominated TV and the headlines from 1950 to his downfall in 1954. Never producing the proofs he claimed he had, he accused the State Department, the Defense Department, the CIA, and other agencies of sheltering scores of Communist agents. For years few dared to speak out against him. Even powerful figures in public life feared to tangle with him. The first to challenge him was the only woman then in the Senate, Margaret Chase Smith of Maine. She too had kept silent for months, expecting McCarthy to produce some solid evidence. But as his accusations grew ever more reckless, she took the Senate floor. In firm tones she said to the silent, crowded chamber:

I think that it is high time for the United States Senate to do some real soul searching. . . . Those of us who shout the loudest about Americanism in making character assassinations are all too frequently those who, by our own words and acts, ignore some of the basic principles of Americanism—

The right to criticize.

The right to hold unpopular beliefs.

The right to protest.

The right of independent thought.

The exercise of those rights should not cost one single American citizen his reputation or his right to a livelihood, nor should he be in danger of losing his reputation or livelihood merely because he happens to know someone who holds unpopular beliefs. Who of us does not? Otherwise none of us could call our souls our own. Otherwise thought control would have set in.

The American people are sick and tired of being afraid to speak their minds lest they be politically smeared as Communists or Fascists by their opponents. Freedom of speech is not what it used to be in America. It has been so abused by some that it is not exercised by others. . . .

Five years after his rise the Senate, at last, said McCarthy had gone too far. A Senate committee held hearings to look into the charge that his conduct was unbecoming a senator. The hearings were televised to the nation in 1954; millions were stunned by McCarthy's tactics in defending himself. The sneering, the bullying of witnesses, the unprovable and ridiculous attacks on respected citizens, his cruelty and recklessness, shocked many who had once supported or tolerated him.

The hearings destroyed McCarthy. A large Senate majority publicly condemned him. His reign of terror was over. He died in obscurity in 1957.

But McCarthyism did not die with him. Committees animated by the inquisitor's spirit continued to examine people's beliefs, to question their loyalty, and to suppress their dissent. The First Amendment—a piece of paper no matter how sanctified—does not by itself guarantee our liberties. If the Bill of Rights is to be enforced, it needs an alert public opinion, it needs a vigilant press, it needs concerted political action to make our freedoms secure.

11
SECRECY AND CENSORSHIP

Attempts in the distant past to curb free expression were not uncommon, as we've seen. What about censorship in more recent times? The very word makes us think of a police state where writers are gagged or deported, editors are jailed, books are banned or burned, and dissenters are sent to labor camps.

Americans who remember so little of our history think censorship is what happens somewhere else. Latin America, yes; China, yes; the Soviet Union, yes; South Africa, yes; but here in the U.S.A.? How could censorship operate in a country protected by the Bill of Rights?

But it did, in the past, and it does, right now.

Recall the two-sided aspect of the American tradition: freedom, and the witch-hunt. A fervid commitment to personal liberties, and a fierce intolerance of unorthodox opinions.

During the 1980s, the very time when the bicentennial of the Constitution was being celebrated, the

Reagan administration and conservative social groups succeeded in narrowly limiting the range of public discussion. Tolerance of diverse views was shoved aside for conformity and "national security."

Parading under the banner of patriotism, high government officials:

- Threatened leading newspapers with criminal prosecution for publishing sensitive information.

- Conducted a massive program of surveillance against groups protesting the administration's policy in Central America.

- Forced hundreds of thousands of federal officials and employees of government contractors to sign secrecy agreements that subjected them to criminal sanctions.

In the 1980s domestic spying on dissident groups and individuals increased considerably. Organizations concerned with the issue of nuclear armaments were harassed by wiretaps, burglaries, tax audits, and infiltration. The familiar intelligence-gathering methods of the FBI and other agencies were now enhanced by massive computer databases. Among the hundreds of activist groups targeted by the government for surveillance were the Maryknoll Sisters, the United Church of Christ, and the United Automobile Workers.

Earlier, in the years of the Nixon administration, investigations by the press and by Congress revealed a widespread pattern of aggressive disruption by the federal government of legitimate political activities. A senate committee headed by Frank Church found evidence that thousands of law-abiding citizens had been the victims of illegal wiretaps and break-ins. The committee concluded, "Domestic intelligence has threatened and undermined the constitutional rights of Americans to free speech, association and privacy. It has done so primarily because the constitutional system for checking abuse of power has not been applied."

Private groups complement whatever government does in violation of the Bill of Rights. They too collect information about people whose political views differ from their own. They operate outside the legal limits placed (however ineffectual) upon government agencies. Some of them have assembled computerized databases on millions of citizens. They create the impression that a nationwide network of dissidents menaces national security and justifies such spying tactics.

It is unreasonable to expect the government to publicly disclose every bit of information it has. Some facts need to be withheld. In time of war the disclosure of military strategy could be disastrous. When governments conduct diplomacy, ill-timed revelation of negotiating positions could be harmful to international relations. Yet secrecy can become addictive. The government officials who plan and execute policy are often prone to operate secretly. The less the people know, the less likely it is anyone will criticize or interfere with their projects. They fear public disapproval or they believe they know best; what the people don't know can't hurt them. That desire to work behind closed doors ought to be controlled, especially in the American system which prides itself on the openness of its democracy.

Uncalled-for secrecy in government was not unknown in earlier times. A powerful accelerator of it came during World War II, when the program to build the first atomic bomb was launched with the greatest secrecy. Not even Congress was allowed to know, nor was Roosevelt's vice president, Harry Truman. A vast research and production apparatus was set up, employing tens of thousands of people, and operating under its own rules. Extreme penalties were threatened for violating the secrecy.

The bombs destroyed Hiroshima and Nagasaki and the war ended. But the secrecy did not. Private industry too, taking part in nuclear power development, came under the same cloak of secrecy. Even when nuclear energy had become a commercial enterprise and was no longer a state secret, the secrecy system and the self-censorship that went with it continued. The precedent had been set: It was all right for the government to place strict controls on information.

Censorship is of course the other face of secrecy. Secrecy permits the centralization of power, and censorship protects power from those who would criticize it. It was that desire to limit the free expression of dissent that rose on the tide of anti-Communist feeling when the Cold War began.

One aspect of censorship ought to be mentioned. That is censorship in America's schools and libraries. It is nothing new: The struggle over the contents of children's and young adults' reading materials began in colonial times. Quaker books were banned in the Massachusetts Bay Colony. Censorship then, as now, is the consequence of what various groups think American society should be like. They want to mold the youth to the group's own image. But in recent years censorship has intensified. Books, films, classroom courses, and student publications have been removed, banned, and even burned by parents and pressure groups who consider them dangerous. The freedom to inquire, to learn, to know, is what is really in great danger. And so are the students' rights to free speech and expression. The attacks on First Amendment liberties come from almost all parts of the country, and are often planned by national groups.

When the public school system was created in the nineteenth century, one of its primary goals was the assimilation of the many diverse peoples who migrated to America, and the teaching of toleration for all. Democratic values, yes, but they conflict with what many parents wish. And that is to have their children exposed only to their own particular religious and moral views.

As a result classroom instruction for generations was rather bland and complacent. School officials wished to offend no one, and textbooks conformed to that desire. America was perfect, children were told, the greatest nation on earth, and the ultimate expression of freedom, democracy, and technological progress.

Things began to change as social tensions erupted

in the years after World War II. The Supreme Court called for desegregation of the schools in 1954, and in 1963 it affirmed the secular nature of state-sponsored schools by banning the recitation of prayers in public schools.

These two landmark cases signaled that a transformation of public education was under way. Congress soon voted massive funds for aid to the schools. The aim was to improve opportunities for all groups—racial and ethnic minorities and the disabled—whose needs had been neglected for so long. Curriculum and textbooks were modified too. Greater openness and honesty about the American past entered the classroom. America in all its multicultural diversity, with its faults as well as its achievements, was portrayed.

"Young adult books until about 1967 were generally safe, pure and simplistic," note professors Kenneth Donelson and Aileen Nilsen in their book *Literature for Today's Young Adults*. "They were devoid of the reality that young people faced daily—violence, pregnancy, premarital sex, profanity, drinking, smoking, abortion, runaways, alienation, the generation gap, suicide, death, prejudice, poverty, class distinctions, drugs, divorce, and on and on."

But in the late sixties, fiction and nonfiction began to appear that were both honest and popular with the young. Reading lists stretched to include many of these titles. They depicted young people who asked questions of their parents, who had doubts and conflicts over moral and ethical issues, and who sometimes went astray. Teachers were encouraged to design their courses to introduce materials that opened up discussion of their communities, their families, their society. This was what a school should be: a "place where freedom to think and to inquire is protected, where all sorts of ideas can be considered, analyzed, investigated, discussed, and their consequences thought through." These are the words of two educators at Arizona State University. The primary right of students is to learn, and the function of the school is to teach them how to think.

This movement in the schools toward a more critical approach to the world alarmed some parents. They regarded it as a challenge to authority and a danger to traditional moral and religious values. To them, open-ended discussion and independent thinking were threatening. Some of the new textbooks and some of the books on reading lists were tarred as "antireligious" or "dirty." Censorship spread widely and rapidly.

A detailed study of censorship efforts, written by Donna A. Demac and published in 1988 by the PEN American Center, reported this situation:

The range of objectionable material cited by the textbook crusaders is vast. Aside from their insistence that the biblical story of creation be granted at least equal status with evolution in describing the origins of human life, they have been militant about any text that reflects the social transformation of the past thirty years. The movements for civil rights, women's liberation, and disarmament are all suspect. Anything that veers from traditional perspectives on sexuality, social roles, parental authority, and a wide variety of other such matters is considered taboo. Sometimes a whole text is considered objectionable; in other cases only particular passages are specified as offensive. "Dangerous" words and phrases have been found in dictionaries, nursery rhymes, the works of Shakespeare, and home economics texts.

A 1988 survey by Dr. Lee Burress of the University of Wisconsin listed these titles as the ones most frequently challenged:

1. *The Catcher in the Rye* by J. D. Salinger
2. *The Grapes of Wrath* by John Steinbeck
3. *Of Mice and Men* by John Steinbeck
4. *Go Ask Alice* (anonymous)
5. *Forever . . .* by Judy Blume
6. *Our Bodies, Ourselves* by the Boston Women's Health Collective
7. *The Adventures of Huckleberry Finn* by Mark Twain
8. *The Learning Tree* by Gordon Parks
9. *My Darling, My Hamburger* by Paul Zindel
10. *1984* by George Orwell
11. *Black Boy* by Richard Wright
12. *The Canterbury Tales* by Geoffrey Chaucer
13. *Slaughterhouse-Five* by Kurt Vonnegut

Glance at the record of what most often comes under fire, and it is plain that any work might be censorable. Someone somewhere is sure not to like it. A particular book will infuriate some people and enthrall others. But let any one book be forced out of a classroom or library, and what book will be safe thereafter?

Parents who challenge books no doubt have what they consider to be good intentions. Isn't that outweighed by the reality that the censorship they invoke is harmful to free expression and good education? Kurt Vonnegut (on the list above) puts it this way: "Can the Constitution of the United States be made a scrap of paper by appeals to what sincere persons believe the laws of God and nature to be?" The American Library Association, the National Council of Teachers of English, the Authors' Guild, PEN, and many other groups have long been on record against censorship.

The constitutional rights of public-school students were weakened by a Supreme Court decision in 1988. "Previously the Court had allowed administrators to inflict corporal punishment without notice or a hearing, to search lockers on little more than a hunch and to punish students for school election speeches containing mild double entendres," wrote Professor Herman Schwartz of the American University law school. "In *Hazelwood v. Kuhlmeier* the Court granted administrators very broad authority to censor school newspapers. Students in a Missouri high school journalism class who published a newspaper had scheduled stories on teenage pregnancy and on the effects of divorce on children. The principal refused to allow the stories to be published and ripped out two whole pages of the paper. A 5–3 majority approved his action, upholding censorship when 'reasonably related to pedagogical concerns,' which gives principals virtually unlimited censorship authority."

The Court left unclear whether it might sanction censorship of college newspapers. A study of the question was financed by the Gannett Foundation and made by Professor Ivan Holmes of the University of Arkansas. He visited eighteen colleges to gauge the extent of press censorship. He concluded, "The censorship dragon is alive and well on university campuses throughout the United States."

In Washington the Student Press Law Center reported receiving more than 550 calls in 1988 from student journalists complaining about censorship. Mark Goodman, the center's executive director, said, "An increasing number of school officials are taking advantage of the Supreme Court's broad language [in *Hazelwood*] and censoring student viewpoints simply because they disagree with them."

One response to increased censorship of the official student press has been the appearance of underground newspapers. A case arose in the state of Washington that reached the Court of Appeals of the Ninth Circuit. The judges ruled unanimously that such a paper that "enriches the school environment for students" is beyond restraint by school principals.

A few things might be said about common misunderstandings of what free expression means. One is that it is wrong to identify a position for freedom of speech with advocacy of the particular subject that the speech concerns. To defend a person's right to express an unpopular opinion does not mean you agree with that position. You are only defending the First Amendment right to free speech.

Another mistaken notion is that the First Amendment was designed to protect the press as a "neutral" forum for "balanced" discussion. To the contrary: Madison and the Congress meant to protect expression of strong views of every kind: left, right, outrageous, foolish, whatever. The whole idea of free expression is to encourage convictions to be voiced, and leave it to the people to decide what they believe. Of course all sides (there may well be more than two sides) should be heard, but no one book or newspaper or film or TV program is obligated to present all sides. Anyone is free to take a stand. To demand "balance" in every publication leads to self-censorship. The media have an obligation to seek the truth and to bring it out.

It should also be clear that it usually takes money to finance publication of an opinion. That in itself severely limits freedom of expression. The owner of a big newspaper or TV station is much freer to express his or her ideas than the man or woman on the street. The mass media especially, capable of reaching millions every day, dominate the channels of information and ideas. The interests of the powerful owners tend to make news reporting and comment conform to what those interests require. That understandable tendency should make us all a bit skeptical of what we read and see. But if it is any comfort, the fact is that we Americans are not alone in violations of the right to free expression.

Our First Amendment freedoms were incorporated

over forty years ago into the United Nations Declaration of Human Rights. Article 19 reads that "Everyone has the right to freedom of opinion and expression; this right includes freedom to hold opinion without interference and to seek, receive and impart information and ideas through any media regardless of frontiers." But deadly forms of censorship continue in at least fifty countries, according to a 1988 report by the U.N. In Kenya you cannot circulate copies of the Constitution. In Ireland you cannot publish or provide information about abortion. In Iraq you can be executed for insulting the president.

In authoritarian states, says the U.N. report, censorship operates brutally through the assassination, kidnaping, and imprisonment of journalists and dissidents. The licensing and bribing of journalists, and the discriminatory use of economic sanctions and control of production machinery, tame the press as well, making it an arm of the state.

And in Western democracies? The report says subtler methods are used to curb dissent: by official-secrets laws, by banning the publication and discussion of information considered harmful to national security, by laws pertaining to libel, defamation, and obscenity.

One can only conclude that people suffer almost everywhere for holding contrary opinions and for trying to express them. Governments of all political hues deny access to information that people have a need and right to know.

12

A NATION OF JOINERS

It was not by accident that the First Amendment rights to freedom of speech and the press were coupled in a single guarantee with "the right of the people peaceably to assemble, and to petition the government for redress of grievances." All these, not by coincidence, are inseparable.

In his classic 1835 study *Democracy in America*, Alexis de Tocqueville, a liberal French politician who traveled in the United States, said, "In no country in the world has the principle of association been more successfully used or applied to a greater multitude of objects than in America." He wrote that more than 150 years ago, but it is even more true today. Americans are and always have been great joiners. There are hundreds of thousands of associations, organizations, clubs, societies, lodges, fraternities, political parties, social groups, and ad hoc committees formed for specific causes. It is a prodigious array of interest groups without equal anywhere else.

No wonder, then, that the right of association has a firm place in American constitutional law. It is natural for you to want to act for yourself, and then to combine your efforts with people of like mind to act in concert with them. Natural as it seems, it is a right often regarded as dangerous. In the sixteenth and seventeenth centuries dissident churches were attacked as subversive, as were labor unions from the eighteenth century into the twentieth.

The right of people to assemble for lawful purposes and to petition existed long before the Constitution was adopted. The English barons demanded it of the king at the time of the Magna Carta. During our own revolutionary period the Stamp Act Congress of 1765 asserted "the right of the British subjects in these colonies to petition the King or either House of Parliament." The First Continental Congress in 1774 did the same, and two years later the Declaration of Independence reaffirmed the right when it said that "our repeated Petitions have been answered only by repeated Injury." The new constitutions of the revolutionary states spelled out a guarantee of rights to assemble and petition. And those rights became part of the First Amendment ratified in 1791.

How well could democracy function if we did not have the right to assemble and petition? It would be a hollow political system if citizens could not gather to exchange ideas and information and seek support for their views and complaints. When the right to petition for changes to meet the needs of society is denied, the situation becomes politically explosive. Recall how the Southerners in the House of Representatives had a gag rule passed that in effect set aside all petitions against slavery. That violation of a basic right so angered people hitherto indifferent to abolition that many joined the cause. They realized that destruction of civil liberty for one group could lead to the destruction of civil liberty for all.

The movement for women's rights that fired the hopes of thousands of supporters in the mid-1800s is another example of the need for people to assemble peaceably to petition the government for redress of grievances. Susan B. Anthony and Elizabeth Cady Stanton set to work to abolish New York's discriminatory laws against women. They knew the state legislature would not listen to a few voices crying for justice. So they held meetings in many parts of the state to educate women and through them organized a massive petition campaign. They collected so many names that in 1860 the legislature changed the law. Women would now have control of their property and their earnings and joint control with their husbands over their children. The lawmakers gave women the right to sue if injured and the right to make contracts or agreements.

That experience in petitioning was applied during the Civil War to the campaign for a constitutional amendment that would permanently free all slaves. Through the efforts of the Women's National Loyal Union 400,000 signatures were gathered and presented to Congress; it helped mightily to get the Thirteenth Amendment passed and ratified. The rights to assemble and petition moved to another stage when women used them to win the vote for themselves through the Nineteenth Amendment.

The word "peaceably" in the First Amendment means that under some circumstances government may place some rules around those rights. Liberty does not mean that lawless acts will be tolerated. The freedom to assemble does not permit a group to destroy the lives, liberties, or property of others. If a mob assembles to lynch a man, it does not have the protection of the First. Nor does a crowd being whipped up by a speaker trying to start a riot.

You would think working people in a free country would have some say about what pay they would accept and what hours they would work. But it took great pressure on employers for that to happen. The right of labor to associate was treated as an illegal combination or a conspiracy contrary to the public interest. Ignoring the First Amendment, the courts suppressed trade unions as they attempted to organize early in the 1800s. Gradually, over a long period of time, the right of workers to organize was recognized. In 1935 the Wagner Labor Relations Act declared it was the policy of the United States to encourage collective bargaining and to protect "the exercise by workers of full freedom of association, self-organization and designation of representatives of their own choosing." The Supreme Court held that "union was essential to give laborers opportunity to deal on an equality with employers."

A form of assembly linked to unions—picketing—illustrates how the law tried to balance liberty with order. Workers in unions, or those wanting a union to represent them, sometimes walk in line outside factories or stores, carrying placards with their slogans and demands, shouting, singing, and chanting. People who cross these lines, including strikebreakers hired by the company, might be assailed by boos, insults, and sometimes violence. Picketing, said the Supreme Court in 1940, is a legitimate form of expression protected by the First Amendment. But picketing could be banned in those cases where there were repeated outbreaks of violence. Picketing was lawful if it was peaceful and did not interfere with the rights of others. This was the court's way of reconciling the principles of order and liberty. Sometimes the Court has favored local, state, or federal government restrictions at the cost of individual freedoms, and at other times it has favored the greatest amount of freedom for the individual.

Since the end of World War II and the advent of the Cold War, the government has taken some steps that hamper the right to join freely associations of one's choice. Under pressure of the anti-Communist fever the government began to inquire into the facts of membership in certain kinds of groups. (We saw this process at work in Chapter 10.) Supreme Court majorities made it constitutionally permissible for the state and federal governments to ask people, including public employees, whether they were or had been members of the Communist party or other organizations labeled subversive.

Where such associations and their activities were not deemed subversive, however, the Supreme Court refused to sanction prying into their membership. The right to join such groups was upheld in the case of such civil rights organizations as the National Association for the Advancement of Colored People (NAACP), that spearheaded the drive for equal rights in the South. Some Southern states tried to deny these groups their basic constitutional rights by all sorts of tactics designed to cripple or destroy them.

Without the right of association, the citizen in a modern state as huge and complex as ours would be helpless. How could he act politically and effectively unless free to work in association with others without any hindrance? Government has the obligation to protect the right of association from invasion by others and to refrain from limiting it by its own actions.

It isn't easy to define the boundaries of free association. The right is no more absolute in character than the other rights we cherish, such as freedom of religion or freedom of speech. Private rights may conflict with each other, and sometimes the public interest outweighs private concerns. The Supreme Court has tried to balance the two. How difficult that problem of balance is, is summarized by a constitutional historian, Professor David Fellman:

The importance of the rights of association demands that the law should regard with great suspicion any attempt to denigrate them. Doubts should be resolved in their favor, never against them; the rights of association are the rule; restraints are only exceptions at best, each of them requiring specific and convincing justification. Nevertheless, there are vital public interests in the maintenance of law and order and in restraining criminal conspiracies, and where such interests exist the rights of association must yield. Since the situations posing the problem of drawing the lines are numerous and complex, our courts—and especially the Supreme Court—have a job of obviously formidable proportions on their hands.

13
GUN CONTROL

"It must be remembered that the right to keep and bear arms is not a right given by the United States Constitution."

That statement was made by a federal appeals court in a 1973 case. It will come as a surprise to many Americans. No constitutional right to keep and bear arms? But what about the Second Amendment?

What that amendment says is clear and simple: "A well-regulated militia, being necessary to the security of a free state, the right of the people to keep and bear arms, shall not be infringed."

The amendment never refers to a "right to bear arms" outside the context of a state militia. Yet time and again, for a great many generations, people have tried to claim the right to keep guns by citing the Second Amendment. And time and again the courts have said essentially what the 1973 decision says.

This fact does not seem to deter the millions of Americans, and their lobbyists from the National Rifle

Association, from insisting on their claim to uncontrolled private ownership of guns. Yet every single Second Amendment case in American history denies that claim. The courts consistently rule that the amendment means:

- No one has the right to carry a concealed weapon.

- Congress may regulate the possession of firearms.

- There is no constitutional right "to bear arms for a lawful purpose."

- There is no right at all of *any* individual to bear arms.

In a 1938 case dealing with the rights granted by the Second Amendment, Justice James C. McReynolds, speaking for a unanimous court, said that the Amendment does not guarantee a right to keep and bear a firearm that does not have "some reasonable relationship to the preservation of efficiency of a well-regulated militia."

The purpose of the Second Amendment, as its language clearly shows, is to insure to the states the right to maintain an armed militia. It has nothing to do with the personal ownership of guns, as the courts have repeatedly held. It only prohibits the federal government from interfering with the state militia. The power of governments—federal, state, local—to strictly regulate the possession of guns is legally unquestionable.

The people who argue against gun-control laws assert that political freedom and personal safety depend upon the ability of persons to defend themselves from tyrants and attackers. But if the private possession of guns ever protected anyone, today it offers only violence. In the age of modern weapons, of high-tech armaments, the individual citizen is helpless against a hostile army. Can a shotgun or assault rifle match a tank, a jet bomber, a hydrogen bomb? Armed civilians are a meaningless defense against a professional military power.

Nor can guns in the hands of private citizens protect them from criminals. To rely on that is to invite anarchy, not law and order; it is to opt for a jungle where each animal depends on itself for survival. "The wrong people survive," said Attorney General Ramsey Clark, "because the calculating killer or the uninhibited psychotic more often wields the faster gun. The average citizen with a gun, acting in self-defense—housewife, bus driver, liquor store clerk—is a greater danger to himself and innocent people in the vicinity than is the crime he would prevent. There are bodies of good people in cemeteries all over the nation which evidence this fact."

What does happen when people own guns and keep them around the house? The journalist Letty Cottin Pogrebin researched the facts, and says these are the likely scenarios:

• They shoot a lover or spouse in the heat of a quarrel, or are shot themselves.

- They are overwhelmed by a stronger assailant who turns the gun against them.

- Their child finds the gun and thinks it is a toy.

- They hear noises, panic, forget all safety instructions, and shoot someone who is not an intruder.

- They overreact and shoot someone who could have been verbally restrained or pacified.

- They shoot when they could have chosen to escape.

- They shoot and harm an innocent bystander.

- Their gun discharges accidentally, or misfires.

- They get depressed and shoot themselves.

These disasters occur thousands of times a year.

There are laws in some states that control certain kinds of weapons. New York, for instance, has tight restrictions on the ownership of concealable hand guns. No one, with certain exceptions, can own a pistol or revolver unless he has first obtained a license. Gun dealers must also be licensed. Getting a license is not easy. The applicant's character and his declared need to have a gun are investigated. He is interviewed and fingerprinted, and both the state and the FBI check on whether he has a criminal record. The state also checks whether the applicant has had a mental illness.

Such laws help to save lives, but so long as a criminal can obtain weapons more easily in other states, by mail order or by going across the state line, the blockage of illicit weapons can't be complete. State gun laws are often and easily evaded.

Because of inadequate federal regulations, a huge number of cheap imported weapons enter the United States. And discarded military weapons are dumped on the American market at low prices.

One type of weapon, the automatic rifle, often called a machine gun, fires a continuous stream of bullets from attached magazines or drums as long as the gun's trigger is pressed. These have been federally banned for civilian sale and ownership, with few exceptions, since the mid-1930s.

Another type of gun, buyable all over America, is the semiautomatic weapon. It fires one bullet with each pull of the trigger but can fire fifty or sixty shots from a magazine without reloading. Its sale and civilian use in the United States has been legal but subject to some restrictions by state or city codes.

In the late 1980s a public controversy flared over government moves to make illegal the importation of these assault rifles and possibly their domestic manufacture too. It is the semiautomatic or assault rifle that a psychotic man used to kill five children in a California schoolyard early in 1989. The same kind of gun is favored by the inner-city drug dealers and the youth gangs. You don't have to be a fellow gangster to be shot in the drug wars. At least 10,000 people per year were killed in the late 1980s, and many were innocent passersby casually gunned down in the spray of bullets.

Yet for all too many years Congress has done little to make it harder for mentally disturbed people and criminals to walk into a store, hand over some money, and go out with an assault rifle meant for soldiers, not civilians. The police nationwide are unanimously for banning such weapons. And the public is beginning to see that certain types of guns must be strictly controlled. They are learning that to do so will not violate the Second Amendment, nor will it prevent civilians from going duck and deer hunting or target shooting with guns that are intended for these sports.

14

THE RIGHT TO BE
LET ALONE

"No soldier shall, in time of peace, be quartered in any house, without the consent of the owner; nor in time of war, but in a manner to be prescribed by law."

That's how the Third Amendment reads. When it was drafted, the experience of the colonial period was still bitter in everyone's mind. The Boston Tea Party had enraged the British, and Parliament and George III felt the people of the town must be punished, or the lawlessness would spread through the colonies. So in 1774 measures were taken (the colonists called them the Intolerable Acts) directed against Massachusetts. The redcoats up to then had been living in tents on the Boston Common. Now, under the Quartering Act, commanders could force citizens to house troops in their homes.

For the new nation just liberated from British rule, the prohibition stated in the Third Amendment made sense. But why was it needed after the British were thrown out? Because revolutionary Americans continued to fear what their own government might do. Even when foreign soldiers were no longer a problem, many Americans could not be sure what a powerful federal government might impose upon them. The Third, then, is a "just-in-case" right. It has never had to be invoked. Today the armed forces have ample quarters of their own. People are not ordered to put them up in their homes.

But if man's home is his castle, it needs still other protection. That's what the Fourth Amendment adds. When police officers want to enter your home and search your possessions, they must first get a warrant. That is a legal document issued by a magistrate, authorizing them to do so. Officers cannot get a warrant to do this just because they suspect you've done something wrong. They have to show a magistrate that there is a "probable cause" for action.

The Fourth Amendment reads:

The right of the people to be secure in their persons, houses, papers, and effects, against unreasonable searches and seizures, shall not be violated, and no warrants shall issue but upon probable cause, supported by oath or affirmation, and particularly describing the place to be searched, and the persons or things to be seized.

Like the other amendments, this right can be traced back to injustices suffered by the colonists. In the 1700s the British government permitted judges to issue "general writs of assistance." With such writs British agents could search any place, day or night, to try to find contraband goods. The colonists argued such writs violated their rights. The freedom of one's home was essential to personal liberty.

The Fourth has two parts. One requires that searches and seizures shall be "reasonable"; the other requires specific warrants. Simple, it would seem, but precisely what the Fourth means has been argued fiercely in the law courts. Many inconsistencies developed in the views of courts and the police as to what is allowable and what is not allowable under the Fourth. Originally the Fourth, like the other parts of the Bill of Rights, was applied only to matters coming under federal jurisdiction. The Fourteenth Amendment, as we have seen, extended these protections to judicial proceedings in the states.

Without the Fourth Amendment, citizens can be the victims of tactics by the police like those experienced by Germany and occupied Europe when the Nazis held power. Millions of people were seized in their homes and dragged off to concentration camps. The same was true even earlier in the Soviet Union and is still the practice in totalitarian regimes in many parts of the world.

In America too that kind of arbitrary intrusion by the police or other government agents has occurred in the past and still occurs. Unlawful authority has been used not only in criminal cases but to combat political dissent as well. Earlier we encountered some of these approaches—government secrecy laws, the resort to emergency measures, the requirement of loyalty oaths, and secret surveillance of suspect persons or groups.

A major tool of the executive branch in political

cases has been wire or electronic surveillance, with little concern for the Fourth Amendment's requirements, such as probable cause. It has often been done by asserting the executive branch's power to protect national security. It places before the courts the issue of deciding what, if any, particular alleged threat to national security justifies the use of extraconstitutional measures.

In a 1972 decision the Court rejected the government's claim that it had broad national security power; it ruled that surveillance of a domestic group that had no connection to a foreign power could not be carried on without a legal warrant.

In one of the famous decisions upholding the Fourth Amendment, Justice Felix Frankfurter, speaking for the majority, said:

> *The knock at the door, whether by day or by night, as a prelude to a search, without authority of law but solely on the authority of the police, did not need the commentary of recent history to be condemned as inconsistent with the conception of human rights enshrined in the history and basic constitutional documents of English-speaking peoples.*

Frankfurter added, however, that evidence taken unconstitutionally could be used against an accused person in a state criminal court. Although, he went on, if officers did that, they could be reprimanded or sued for damages.

Dissenting to this aspect, Justice Frank Murphy said that "but one remedy exists to deter violations of the search and seizure clause. That is the rule which excludes illegally obtained evidence. Only by exclusion can we impress upon the zealous prosecutor that violation of the Constitution will do him no good."

The exclusionary rule was first applied to federal courts some seventy-five years ago. Critics claim it deprives the courts of important evidence in criminal cases. The rule does prevent certain evidence from coming before a court. That's because there are other values as important as convicting the accused. A confession to a priest or a lawyer might determine guilt, but the legal system forgoes such evidence because it respects conscience and legal rights. In 1914 the Supreme Court declared the exclusionary rule essential to constitutional order. It warned that courts must not be accomplices to violations. The justices said:

> *The efforts . . . to bring the guilty to punishment, praiseworthy as they are, are not to be aided by the sacrifice of those great principles established by years of endeavor and suffering which have resulted in their embodiment in the fundamental law of the land.*

More recently, the Supreme Court has allowed the "good faith" exception when an officer obtains a search warrant that proves to be defective. At least this decision recognized the importance of securing a warrant. Still, accepting "good faith" is like saying a policeman may violate the law so long as he means well. Such a standard makes it easier for officers to avoid the consequences of violating the Constitution.

It's a dangerous line to cross. How can it be proved or disproved that someone acted in "good faith?"

The right to privacy in one's home falls under the Fourth Amendment. Justice Louis D. Brandeis, in an oft-quoted dissent of 1928, said, "The makers of our Constitution . . . conferred, as against the Government, the right to be let alone—the most comprehensive of rights and the right most valued by civilized men. To protect that right, every unjustifiable intrusion by the Government upon the privacy of the individual, whatever the means employed, must be deemed a violation of the Fourth Amendment."

When the Fourth was adopted and until fairly recently, a person's records were kept either in the home or the place of business. The Fourth limits the government's power to search those premises, in order to protect your privacy.

Under modern conditions much of your personal data is now maintained in a great many other places— schools, hospitals, banks, insurance companies, motor vehicle bureaus, the Internal Revenue Service, credit agencies, employers, the Social Security Administration. They all keep files on many aspects of your life and activities. And through the use of your individual Social Security number, what one data bank holds about you is linked to all the others by computer tapes.

How does this affect your right to privacy? The Supreme Court hasn't applied the Fourth to such information kept by third parties. Ironically, you are still protected in the home or place of business, although the information the Fourth was meant to keep private for you either is no longer there or is also in a lot of other places. The result is that government officials can get their hands on highly personal information, without bothering to get legal permission to enter your home and search it.

It is in the courts that most civil liberties issues are decided, and the courts, as we've seen, may shift position, now approving, now disapproving. The Warren Court gave a broad reading to the Fourth. It required suppression of illegally obtained evidence in state prosecutions, and demanded that judicial approval be obtained in advance of all searches, unless compelling circumstances made this impossible. (Who defines "compelling circumstances"?) It ruled too that electronic surveillances (wiretapping or more advanced methods) were "searches" under the Fourth and needed the same prior judicial approval.

But the Supreme Court under Chief Justice Warren Burger diminished these protections. It held that we couldn't expect privacy in personal bank accounts, that the phone company could make our records available to the police; and it gave law enforcement free rein to use informers and agents. In other words, the government could infiltrate your home and your life with spies, although it could not freely rummage through your drawers or tap your phone.

In one decision, *United States v. White* (1971), the Court held that a government informer, without warrant or other court order, could engage a person in conversations that are transmitted by concealed radio to federal agents. The Fourth, it ruled, did not protect a defendant who trusts an apparent colleague when that colleague is a government agent informing the authorities of what he hears. The Court assumed only "wrongdoers" would be risking arrest by placing their confidence in police agents.

Justice Harlan, dissenting, asserted that the issue isn't simply whether criminals place unjustified reliance on so-called friends. He said that opinion missed the mark entirely:

> *The interest [to be protected] is the expectation of the ordinary citizen, who has never engaged in illegal conduct in his life, that he may carry on his private discourse freely, openly, and spontaneously without measuring his every word against the connotations it might carry when instantaneously heard by others unknown to him and unfamiliar with his situation or analyzed in a cold, formal record played days, months, or years after the conversation.*

15

THE RIGHT TO REMAIN SILENT

And now we come to the Fifth Amendment, the most varied of all. It became the bulwark of the accusatorial system of criminal justice and the mainstay of First Amendment freedoms. What does it do?

- It guarantees grand jury proceedings before you can be put to trial for a serious offense.

- It bans double jeopardy.

- It protects against compulsory self-incrimination.

- It requires due process of law before you can be deprived of life, liberty, or property.

- It assures you of just compensation if government takes your private property.

It is the clause that guarantees the right not to incriminate yourself that will be discussed here. The other parts of the Fifth, easier to grasp, were described earlier.

The newspapers often print headlines like these:

TWO DECLINE TO TALK AT CRIME HEARINGS

JOHN DOE PLEADS FIFTH IN U.S. INQUIRY

JANE DOE'S APPEAL TO FIFTH AMENDMENT
BLOCKS SENATE INVESTIGATION

LAWYER ADVISES ACCUSED
OF RIGHT TO REMAIN SILENT

Although the circumstances may vary widely, each witness resorted to the right to remain silent. Why a right to remain silent? We know what the First Amendment right to freedom of speech means. But why do we need a right *not* to speak?

The words simply mean that we cannot be made to testify against ourselves. We have the right to remain silent when called before a criminal or civil court, a grand jury, a legislative inquiry, or virtually any other form of official investigation. (Lawyers call it "the right against self-incrimination.")

The origins of this right go back in English law at least to the Middle Ages, but the principle is even older. The Talmud of ancient Babylon said that a man need not "put himself in the place of the guilty one." And in the account of Jesus' trial given in Matthew 26, we read that in answer to one question, Jesus remained silent, and to another replied, "*Thou* has said."

Why should an innocent person refuse to answer questions? Surely he has nothing to hide. Don't those who refuse have something to hide? If a person has done nothing illegal, how can just telling the truth hurt him?

The right to remain silent was put into the Bill of Rights as a protection the Constitution offers both the innocent and the guilty. The men who wrote the Fifth knew from history that innocent people are often accused of crimes and sometimes falsely convicted.

That innocent people *are* convicted in American courts today too is reported in the newspapers all too often. Such a case was made the subject of a documentary film in 1988—*The Thin Blue Line*, by Errol Morris. Partly as the result of the film's exposure of the truth and of a defense lawyer's long struggle to prove his client's innocence, a man convicted of murder in Texas was freed in 1989, after many years in prison.

In his book called *Convicting the Innocent*, Yale law professor Edwin M. Borchard describes sixty-five cases, culled from what he said were a much larger number, in which innocent people had been convicted. Among them were men and women who had been forced into confession, including confession of murder.

It is possible for an innocent person to give testimony that would help a prosecutor prove a case against him. Witnesses who know they have committed no crime nevertheless realize that their own testimony might place themselves in danger. It was for such situations that the Fifth Amendment was particularly designed.

The claim to this right to remain silent stems from the principle that the accused is entitled to fair play. Leonard Levy, the foremost authority on the Fifth, explains the cluster of principles out of which the right emerged:

> It harmonized with the principles that the accused was innocent until proved guilty and that the burden of proof was on the prosecution. It was related to the idea that a man's home should be not promiscuously broken into and rifled for evidence of his reading and writing. It was intimately connected to the belief that torture or cruelty in forcing a man to expose his guilt was unfair and illegal. It was indirectly associated with the right to have witnesses on behalf of the defendant, so that his lips could remain sealed against the government's questions or accusations. . . .
>
> The right became . . . one of the ways of fairly determining guilt or innocence, like trial by jury itself; it became part of due process of the law, a fundamental principle of the accusatorial system. It reflected the view that society benefits by seeking the defendant's conviction without the aid of his involuntary admissions. Forcing self-incrimination was thought to brutalize the system of criminal justice and to produce untrustworthy evidence. Above all, the right was closely linked to freedom of speech and religious liberty.

Bear in mind that the Constitution guarantees all of us the right of freedom of religion, speech, press, assembly, and petition. That's the First Amendment. Yet we saw, in Chapter 10, how again and again people in power seek to stamp out religious, political, or any other form of dissent they regard as a danger. Investigating committees set themselves up as both accuser and judge and try to force witnesses to confess to radical or unpopular views, and so discredit and punish them.

Some who were accused of being Communists and denied it were tried for perjury and sometimes convicted on the testimony of witnesses who were later discovered to be liars or who admitted to it. So the last recourse for those who wished to protect their beliefs and associations from this kind of inquisition was to use the right to remain silent.

Old as the right to remain silent is in the American tradition, its roots go far deeper in history, back to the days long, long ago when our ancestors thought that torturing a suspect or a witness was a good way to get people to accuse themselves. The ancient Egyptians did it; so did the Greeks and Romans. And in the time of the Inquisition, so did the Christian Church. In the twentieth century it has been a method commonly used in totalitarian societies. Even now the practice of torture exists in many parts of the world.

The best way to get at the truth, such "experts" believed, was to obtain a confession. If the accused will not agree to speak, then stretch him on the rack till his bones break, crush his thumbs, pull out his nails, beat him to a pulp—and his confession will come. Of course most people put to such torture will confess to anything to end the terrible ordeal.

The principle of the Fifth Amendment right to remain silent we owe largely to one man, John Lilburne, an English pamphleteer who devoted his life to the cause of liberty and democracy. In 1637 he defied a Royal Star Chamber—the name for the king's privy council when it sat as a court to try cases of disobedience to royal orders—when he was tried on a charge of printing and publishing seditious books. He affirmed a right not to incriminate himself when he said, "I am not willing to answer to you any more of these questions, because I see you go about this examination to ensnare me." His courage roused great popular feeling against the whole system of forcing a witness to testify, the system that had victimized him and his Puritan friends. Lilburne's example led to the establishment of the right to remain silent.

That right was carried to the colonies and written into the constitutions of seven of the original thirteen American states, but only after generations of hard struggle to get it accepted. In drafting that clause in the Fifth Amendment of the Bill of Rights, the framers insisted that the enduring interests of the community required justice to be done as fairly as possible. They believed a system of criminal justice should minimize the possibility of convicting an innocent person. And at the same time the law should show humanity even to the offender. "The Fifth Amendment," wrote Professor Levy, "reflected their judgment that in a society based on respect for the individual, the government shouldered the entire burden of proving guilt and the accused need make no unwilling contribution to his conviction."

Many others have shared this belief. In the words of Dean Erwin Griswold of Harvard Law School: The Fifth is "one of the great landmarks in man's struggle to make himself civilized." And Justice William Douglas said: "It is our way of escape from the use of torture. . . . It is part of our respect for the dignity of man."

16

THE PROMISE
OF A FAIR TRIAL

Like the Fifth Amendment, the Sixth, Seventh, and Eighth also deal with the rights of the accused in criminal proceedings. The promise of a fair trial is as ancient as the Mosaic code. The laws handed down by Moses required two witnesses to agree on testimony in order for the accused to be convicted of a major offense. Later the Romans gave accused persons the right to confront their accusers "face to face." And as we noted earlier, the Magna Carta guaranteed that "no freeman shall be taken, or imprisoned, outlawed or exiled, or in any way harmed . . . save by the lawful judgment of his peers or by the law of the land."

The framers of the Bill of Rights wrote the Sixth and Seventh Amendments because they believed in the principle that all men, of whatever station in life, come under the law of the land. So the Sixth begins:

In all criminal prosecutions, the accused shall enjoy the right to a speedy and public trial, by an impartial jury of the state and district wherein the crime shall have been committed, which district shall have been previously ascertained by law . . . .

The brief Seventh Amendment deals with civil actions. It states:

In suits at common law, where the value in controversy shall exceed twenty dollars, the right to trial by jury shall be preserved, and no fact tried by a jury shall be otherwise re-examined in any court of the United States than according to the rules of the common law.

What a jury should be or how a jury trial should be conducted is not spelled out in the Sixth or Seventh. But Supreme Court decisions have held that in federal cases a jury should consist of twelve people, that the trial should be supervised by a judge with power to instruct the jurors on what the law is and advise them on the facts, and that the verdict should be unanimous. In some states and situations, minor crimes and some kinds of civil cases are handled by juries with less than twelve members. States are not compelled to have jury trials at all in civil actions.

In federal courts unanimous verdicts by the jury are required, in both civil and criminal cases. Why unanimous when a simple majority is usually decisive in so many other situations? Because the law calls for establishing the guilt of a defendant beyond any "reasonable doubt." To get a twelve-to-zero vote means that every last one of the jurors has to be convinced by the evidence, or a verdict cannot be rendered. Of course there are "hung juries," which means the twelve could not come to agreement one way or the other, even though they may have spent days or weeks pondering. In some state courts, however, the unanimous rule does not apply for lesser crimes and civil cases. The Supreme Court has not overruled such state constitutional provisions.

Not all cases involving penalties are criminal cases. But generally the more serious offenses are entitled to the protection of the Sixth. "Speedy" doesn't mean persons arrested today must be indicted tomorrow and tried the next day. Delay in the proceedings is often a practical necessity on account of crowded court calendars, too few judges, and unavailable defense counsel. However, a trial can't be delayed for months or years, or the indictment may be dismissed. This right to a speedy trial applies to state as well as federal trials.

A "public" trial allows the press and public to attend. It prevents secret trials (common in totalitarian countries) where a person may be railroaded to jail without anyone even hearing of it.

Juries are required to be "impartial" so that people with a special interest in the case—family, friends of the accused or of the prosecution, business associates, enemies, or people with a strong prejudice in the matter—are not allowed to sit in judgment.

This alone accounts for much time spent by judge, defense counsel, and prosecutor. They question prospective jurors at length about their backgrounds, ideas, and attitudes. Any number of jurors may be eliminated for "cause" by the judge or by lawyers for either side, with the judge's approval. "Peremptory challenges" may also be used, limited in number by law. This means either side making a challenge doesn't have to provide any reason for it, but is simply acting on a feeling that the prospective juror will be prejudiced against their side.

The Supreme Court has declared that an

impartial jury [is] *drawn from a cross section of the community. . . . This does not mean, of course, that every jury must contain representatives of all the economic, social, religious, racial, political, and geographical groups of the community; frequently such complete representation would be impossible. But it does mean that prospective jurors shall be selected by court officials without systematic and intentional exclusion of any of these groups. Recognition must be given to the fact that those eligible for jury service are to be found in every stratum of society. Jury competence is an individual rather than a group or class matter. That fact lies at the very heart of the jury system.*

All citizens are subject to call for jury duty. Although some consider it a bother and are reluctant to give up the time, it is an obligation of citizenship in a democracy that ought to be valued. You get the opportunity to observe how the processes of justice are carried on, and learn to judge your neighbor as you would yourself be judged. It is a lesson in life as well, often life as you have not experienced it yourself.

A trial must take place in the locality where the offense is charged to have been committed. But the accused may request the trial be held in a different district for valid reasons. The media, for instance, may have ignited passions to a point where a fair trial in the community would be impossible.

The Sixth goes on to state that the accused shall "be informed of the nature and cause of the accusation," shall have the right "to be confronted with the witnesses against him," shall "have compulsory process for obtaining witnesses in his favor," and shall "have the assistance of counsel for his defense."

To be informed of the charges gives the accused the chance to make adequate preparation for his defense before the trial begins. At the trial he or his lawyer must be given the opportunity to challenge and cross-examine witnesses who testify against him. If the accused requests it, the state or federal court must order persons into court to testify on his behalf.

This means that the government must make sure that the people who the accused says will be helpful to him as witnesses will appear in court for the trial. The government can issue subpoenas to such people, and if they refuse to come, they are themselves subject to prosecution.

The clause on the right of the accused to counsel for his defense in federal court came out of the time when the common law courts in England refused to let the accused have a defense lawyer. The framers of the Bill of Rights wanted none of that. If the defendant is too poor to afford a lawyer, the federal court must supply a defense attorney at the government's expense.

It was the landmark case of *Gideon v. Wainwright* in 1963 that considerably broadened that right. It happened when Clarence Earl Gideon sent his scrawled petition to the Supreme Court to review his conviction for breaking into a pool parlor in Florida and stealing some money from the bar. He claimed he was unable to afford a lawyer to file his petition for him. He said that at the time of his trial, when he asked for the aid of a lawyer, the court refused him. He was sentenced to five years in prison. He believed that "to try a poor man for a felony without giving him a lawyer was to deprive him of due process of law."

Gideon's appeal was successful, with the help of the American Civil Liberties Union and its appointed lawyer, Abe Fortas, who later became a justice of the Supreme Court. A unanimous Supreme Court ruled that indigent defendants are entitled to lawyers at trial in state courts, as well as federal. Justice Black said:

Reason and reflection require us to recognize that in our adversary system of criminal justice, any person haled into court, who is too poor to hire a lawyer, cannot be assured a fair trial unless counsel is provided for him. This seems to be an obvious truth. Governments, both state and federal, quite properly spend vast sums of money to establish machinery to try defendants accused of crime. Lawyers to prosecute are everywhere deemed essential to protect the public's interest in an orderly society. Similarly, there are few defendants charged with crime, few indeed, who fail to hire the best lawyers they can get to prepare and present their defenses. That government hires lawyers to prosecute and defendants who have the money hire lawyers to defend are the strongest indications of the widespread belief that lawyers in criminal courts are necessities, not luxuries.

Ever since the *Gideon* decision, poor persons in criminal cases have been given lawyers. But lawyers who provide free legal services for the poor have been swamped by the number seeking their help. In 1974 the federal government established a Legal Services Corporation with local offices to provide help in civil cases, but budget cuts by the Reagan administration reduced their staffs everywhere. It crippled the services so that the staff could take on only the cases of people at the most serious legal risk.

A private organization, the Legal Aid Society, offers lawyers for the poor or near poor. Most of its aid goes to criminal cases, although it does provide some help in civil trials too. Civil rights organizations have urged that the *Gideon* right be extended to civil as well as criminal cases. In New York State in the late 1980s the shortage of counsel for the poor was so bad that a state committee appointed by New York's highest court to investigate called it "a blot on our legal system and on our whole society."

The committee urged that the state's 88,000 practicing lawyers be required to devote twenty hours a year to representing the poor in civil cases or pay fifty dollars an hour for another lawyer to perform the twenty hours. A Legal Services lawyer pointed out that such lawyers are not likely to know housing-court procedures or how to maneuver through state and federal bureaucracies to get welfare or Social Security benefits restored for a client. Better if they would contribute money to hire more lawyers experienced in poverty law and who work at much lower rates, he said. One lawyer replied that both contributions and lawyers volunteering their time were needed. "We need a balance, because without obligation to serve the poor our profession suffers."

Another landmark case affecting the rights of the accused was *Miranda v. Arizona*. It arose in 1963, when a young woman was kidnapped and raped near Phoenix, Arizona. Ernesto Miranda, a twenty-three-year-old mentally disturbed man, was arrested soon after. He confessed after two hours of questioning by the police, and was later convicted. His lawyer appealed his conviction. It was argued that the police had not informed Miranda that he had the right to remain silent and the right to be represented by counsel.

In 1966 the Supreme Court, voting five to four, threw out Miranda's confession, holding that the proceeding violated the Fifth and Sixth Amendments, as made applicable to the states by the Fourteenth. The Court spelled out the advice the police must give suspects in custody:

> *Prior to any questioning, the person must be warned that he has a right to remain silent, that any statement he does make may be used against him, and that he has a right to the presence of an attorney, either retained or appointed.*

The Court was saying that the police must make known to the poor and ignorant what is more commonly known to the affluent and the informed. Later, however, the Supreme Court under Chief Justice Burger reduced the scope and effectiveness of the *Miranda* warning. And Congress in 1968 passed a law that in federal cases permitted the use of a voluntary confession even if the accused was not warned of his or her rights. In 1989 the Court ruled five to four that ambiguous instructions given by the police to a murder suspect did not violate the Court's *Miranda* decision.

17

THE LAW SHOULD BE HUMANE

The shortest amendment of all is the Eighth:

Excessive bail shall not be required, nor excessive fines imposed, nor cruel and unusual punishments inflicted.

The aim of the bail provision was to prevent arbitrary imprisonment before trial. When we presume a person to be innocent until convicted of a crime, then the dignity of individuals must not be demeaned by curtailing their liberty through imprisonment unless convicted of a crime. But because bail is asked, however small it be, many poor citizens suffer in jail while awaiting justice. The purpose of bail is to assure that a person charged with crime appears for trial on the date set. He must deposit money, which he forfeits if he does not show up.

The rich and the mobster make bail easily. Only the poor remain in jail. Is that provision in the Eighth fair or just? For the poor who cannot raise bail it means jobs lost, families separated, and the chance to find evidence and witnesses and to prepare a defense gone. Yet thousands of those jailed without bail have been found innocent, the record shows. And hundreds of thousands of others, after long months in jail, have been released without trial. Sometimes they have been jailed longer than a sentence for the alleged crime would have required.

Disturbed by the inequity of the bail requirement for the poor, the Vera Foundation in 1961 launched the Manhattan Bail Project, that has proved a success. It interviews defendants in the criminal court and recommends to the judges the possibility of granting paroles without bail to those individuals whose records indicate they are fairly responsible people. The experiment proved the vast majority would keep their promise to return for trial. Other localities adopted the same policy.

Finally, Congress recognized that defendants should be considered as individuals, not dollar signs. In 1966 it passed a Bail Reform Bill. It specified that the accused be released on his own recognizance when this is justified by past record or by community or family ties. Other alternatives suggested were release in the custody of a person or organization, or release with restrictions: on travel, place of residence, or association.

The clause in the Eighth dealing with cruel and unusual punishment would seem to need little discussion. Behind it is the civilized concern that the law should be humane. To make it humane, "cruel" and "unusual" punishment is barred. A problem arises, however, because people's ideas change about what is cruel or unusual punishment.

The English prohibited it in their Bill of Rights of 1689. They wanted to get rid of the savage sentences handed out by the Star Chamber. Even after the ban was adopted, some punishments by torture and mutilation continued because the courts believed they matched the crime. Later, in the eighteenth century, what seem horrors to us still persisted in England. Criminals might be disemboweled, burned, strangled; they might have their hands or ears cut off, their nostrils slit, their cheeks branded.

In the American colonies, too, punishment was often severe. A robber could be burned on the forehead or hand, flogged, put in the stocks, or branded. With the Revolution some of the states prohibited cruel and unusual punishment, and the framers included the ban in the Eighth Amendment. Still, some people objected: They thought it was necessary to hang villains, or cut off their ears and flog them. Not to do it just because it would be cruel? No, they argued, not until a more lenient way to correct vice is invented.

The first case in which the Supreme Court was asked to rule whether punishment was cruel or unusual came in 1910. And justices decided that the Eighth "is not fastened to the absolute but may acquire meaning as public opinion becomes enlightened by humane practice."

Custom has had a large influence on defining the cruel and unusual. Because flogging or whipping was used for so long, courts upheld the practice. As for the death penalty, back in 1890 the Supreme Court held it was neither cruel nor unusual. At the same time it asserted that the act of execution must be done as swiftly and painlessly as possible.

For a very long time the death penalty was not considered cruel and unusual punishment. Indeed, several states imposed the death penalty for a variety of crimes and allowed juries to decide when the convicted person could be sentenced to death. In 1972 the Supreme Court ruled that because of the arbitrary and capricious manner in which the death penalty was administered in California and certain other states, it was cruel and unusual punishment and therefore unconstitutional. In 1976, however, it changed its mind, reversing itself. Individual states could decide to impose the death penalty for crimes involving special circumstances. The decision put Death Row back in business.

What people who support the death penalty argue is that it stops people from committing capital crimes. But "virtually every study ever made proves that the death penalty has no effect as a deterrent against capital crimes," writes Edmund G. ("Pat") Brown, who as governor of California in 1959–66 let thirty-six people go to their deaths.

Among the facts that helped him change his mind was a study by two law professors published in 1987 in the *Stanford Law Review*. It showed that 350 innocent men had been sentenced to death in the United States in the twentieth century. And twenty-three of them were executed before the mistakes were discovered. The number 350 was a conservative figure, they noted, because they used only cases where the real murderer was found or the state admitted its mistake.

In 1989 the Rehnquist Court, in two separate decisions, ruled that the Constitution permits states to execute murderers who are as young as sixteen when they committed their crimes, as well as those who are mentally retarded.

Of the more than 2,000 people on death row in mid-1989, twenty-seven were sentenced to death for murders committed when they were sixteen and seventeen. No precise figures are available for how many death-row inmates are mentally retarded. But estimates range from one tenth to as much as one third. Of the thirty-seven states that sanctioned the death penalty in 1989, fifteen barred it for those who were under eighteen when they committed capital crimes.

The Court's majority disposed of the last remaining broad-based challenge to the death penalty. Earlier, in 1987, the Court rejected the argument that because those whose murder victims are white are more likely to receive death sentences than those who kill blacks, the death penalty violates the constitutional requirement of equal protection. (About fifty-three percent of all the people executed in America from 1930 to 1965 were black, although blacks were less than ten percent of the population during that period.)

Critics of the recent decisions of the Supreme Court say they mock our proclaimed devotion to human rights. To execute teenagers and individuals with the mental capacity of children is what we would condemn in any other nation. Yet the Supreme Court rules this is sanctioned by the Constitution.

Recent public opinion polls show that an increasing percentage of Americans favors using the death penalty, and more often. Still another sign of change is the decision in some places to jail women for having drug problems when they are pregnant. In Florida in 1989 a woman was convicted of having delivered drugs to a minor—via the umbilical cord. It is a felony drug charge, usually used against dealers, carrying a possible 30-year sentence. In localities in California, New York, Illinois, and Texas women who allegedly used drugs during pregnancy have been charged with prenatal child abuse and neglect.

Yet in 1925 the Supreme Court declared drug addiction to be a medical, not criminal, matter. The Court reiterated this ruling in 1962, stating that "we forget the teachings of the Eighth Amendment if we allow sickness to be made a crime and sick people to be punished for being sick. This age of enlightenment cannot tolerate such barbarous action."

Short of the death penalty, prisoners may suffer cruel and unusual punishment while in confinement. There is ample evidence of barbarous treatment in the distant past, as we've noted. But what about more recently?

For almost a century after the adoption of the Bill of Rights, society believed that prisoners had no rights. The prison inmate was considered "the slave of the state." Not until the 1970s did the judicial system show concern for conditions inside prisons. It was the civil rights and civil liberties movements of the post-World War II decades that woke up the public and the courts. Of course prisoners' rights and civil liberties were reduced when they were jailed. But still, didn't the Constitution apply to them too?

For about ten years the courts examined what went on behind the prison walls. In 1975, for example, a federal court in Alabama studied the entire state prison system. It looked at overcrowding, environmental conditions, idleness, levels of violence, staffing, classification, medical and mental health care, and restrictions on visitation. And it found that the totality of conditions violated the Eighth Amendment's prohibition against cruel and unusual punishment. The court said that "prison conditions are so debilitating that they necessarily deprive inmates of any opportunity to rehabilitate themselves or even maintain skills already possessed." The finding was clear: Prisons make those confined within their walls worse off than when they arrived.

Other state courts followed Alabama's lead. By the early 1980s sixty percent of the states were under similar court investigations. However, it was slow going, for many prison officials, like bureaucrats everywhere, resist change. They prefer things as they are, and public refusal to spend the money required for change makes it hard to carry it out.

It did not help that in the mid-1970s the Supreme Court moved back toward the old era. As Justice Rehnquist remarked about prisoners, "Nobody promised them a rose garden." A majority of the Court in a series of cases was returning to the old "hands-off" doctrine—the belief that prisoners had few or no rights. The Court said that the daily functioning of state prisons was not the business of federal judges.

In 1981 it added that "to the extent that such conditions are restrictive and even harsh, they are part of the penalty that criminals pay for their offenses against society."

What happened in the New Mexico State Penitentiary offers a lesson for every state. In February 1980 the prison exploded in a terrible riot that ended in the death of thirty-three prisoners. In a report ordered by the state legislature, the state attorney general said:

> *Prisons do not deal with the basic problems of crime in our society. Prison is a dehumanizing experience, and most persons come out the worse for being in. Nearly all criminals, even under the strictest sentencing practices, will return to society. Even a well-managed bureaucracy, necessary to run prisons, cannot change these basic truths. . . . If New Mexico's rich heritage of deep familial and community roots is to be realized, communities must play a part in housing, resocializing and accepting persons who have violated the community's laws. If New Mexico does not dramatically change its philosophy and practices about how to deal with criminals, there will be more tragedies. . . . Ultimately, there will be more bureaucracy, more waste of taxpayers' money for architects and buildings, more and more crime and more human waste.*

18

POWERS THAT
BELONG TO THE PEOPLE

The Ninth Amendment isn't easy to grasp, short as it is:

> *The enumeration in the Constitution, of certain rights, shall not be construed to deny or disparage others retained by the people.*

To get at its meaning, recall the thinking of the colonists during the Revolutionary era. Influenced by the ideas of the English philosopher John Locke, many Americans thought that before the institution we call government was established, people lived under "natural law." They conceived of this as an ideal time when humankind had certain rights called natural rights—natural, because they were part of our nature as human beings.

In an essay entitled "The Right to Be Let Alone," Justice Douglas puts it this way:

The natural rights have a broad base in morality and religion to protect man, his individuality, and his conscience against direct and indirect interference by government. Some are written explicitly into the Constitution. Others are to be implied. The penumbra of the Bill of Rights reflects human rights which, though not explicit, are implied from the very nature of man as a child of God. These human rights were the product both of political thinking and of moral and religious influences. Man, as a citizen, had known oppressive laws from time out of mind and was in revolt. Man, as a child of God, insisted he was accountable not to the state but to his own conscience and to his God. Man's moral and spiritual appetite, as well as his political ideals, demanded that he have freedom. Liberty was to be the way of life—inalienable, and safe from intrusion by government. That, in short, was our beginning.

Then, when people agreed with their neighbors to form a political society, they gave up some rights—such as to retaliate against anyone who injured them—in return for protection by the government they had formed. But people retained for themselves other natural rights.

With this in mind, the Americans formed a government and granted certain powers to it through the Constitution. However, to make sure that the government would not interfere with the rights retained by the people, the Bill of Rights was adopted.

This Ninth Amendment was written as an added protection for rights retained by the people, but not named in the other amendments. The advocates of the Ninth believed the listing of natural rights in the first eight amendments did not exhaust all the rights of the people. They wanted to make sure the federal government would not trample on those unlisted rights.

What are those unlisted rights? That's hard to say. They were deliberately not spelled out by the framers who expected that the generations to come would draw out the meaning of these reserved rights to meet the crucial needs of their time. The Supreme Court waited 156 years before it found that a right the government was trying to restrict was protected by the Ninth. This was in the case of the Hatch Act, a law barring federal employees from engaging in certain political activities. In 1947 the Court held that the right to participate in politics was guaranteed by the Ninth Amendment.

Again, in 1965, the Court relied on the Ninth to rule unconstitutional a Connecticut law that made it illegal for married couples to use contraceptive devices for birth control. In the famous case of *Griswold v. Connecticut*, a five-man majority thought that the "right of privacy" (unnamed in the Constitution) had an important bearing on the case. They reasoned that a law making birth control illegal could be policed only by a drastic invasion of a married couple's privacy. That right of privacy, the majority held, was protected by the Ninth. It was a state, not a federal law, so the Court extended the application of the right to states, too.

The right of privacy brought into *Griswold* was also crucial to the controversial ruling in the abortion issue. It was *Roe v. Wade*, the U.S. Supreme Court's 7–2 decision in 1973, holding that the state may not prohibit abortions performed during the first two trimesters of pregnancy. In the *Griswold* opinion, Justice Douglas had shown how the right of privacy emerges from other amendments as well as the Ninth:

> *Various guarantees create zones of privacy. The right of association contained in the penumbra of the First Amendment is one. . . . The Third Amendment in its prohibition against the quartering of soldiers "in any house" in time of peace without the consent of the owner is another facet of that privacy. The Fourth Amendment explicitly affirms the "right of the people to be secure in their persons, houses, papers and effects against unreasonable searches and seizures." The Fifth Amendment in its Self-Incrimination Clause enables the citizen to create a zone of privacy which government may not force him to surrender to his detriment. The Ninth Amendment provides: "The enumeration in the Constitution of certain rights, shall not be construed to deny or disparage others retained by the people."*
>
> *The present case, then, concerns a relationship lying within the zone of privacy created by several constitutional guarantees.*

Roe v. Wade began in Dallas, Texas, when Jane Roe (a fictitious name to shield her privacy), who was an unmarried pregnant woman, wanted an abortion, but the Texas law against abortion stood in her way. She brought suit in federal court challenging the law's constitutionality. Her claim was that the law interfered with her personal right to control her own body. She felt she had a constitutional right to decide this matter for herself.

Justice Harry Blackmun, writing for the majority, found Roe's fundamental right to an abortion in five places in the Constitution. He said it was implied in the First, Fourth, Fifth, Ninth, and Fourteenth amendments. He was reasoning about the right to privacy much as Justice Douglas had in *Griswold*. In other decisions affecting marriage, family, and children the Court had ruled that the Constitution does not allow government to interfere with such personal choices.

The Tenth Amendment was inserted into the Constitution to make clear and certain that the United States of America was a federal government. It reads:

The powers not delegated to the United States by the Constitution, nor prohibited by it to the states, are reserved to the states respectively, or to the people.

These powers not granted to the national government are reserved to the states and to the people. But precisely what are the "reserved" powers? They are not listed. You might try to figure it out by a process of elimination. Start with all the powers given to the national government, plus the powers the states are prohibited from exercising. Then what you have left would be the reserved powers. They seem to fall into such categories as marriage, divorce, and education.

Whatever the reserved powers may be, they do not limit the exercise of the national government's legitimate powers. The Constitution does not explicitly say what the states may do, but does say that no state or local law can be in conflict with the Constitution or with national laws. The major reserved powers of the states are to tax, spend, regulate commerce within the state, and exercise police power.

The Tenth Amendment strengthens the implication that gives value to the Ninth. It says that there are rights and powers that belong to the people, beyond those embraced in state or federal constitutions. These, however they are defined, are not to be infringed by any government.

It seems, then, as Chief Justice Stone said in 1941, that the Tenth Amendment "states but a truism that all is retained which is not surrendered." But it does have value as a signal flag to remind the federal government that its powers have theoretical limits.

AFTERWORD

In the Bill of Rights there are only 462 words. Yet, as Chief Justice Earl Warren once said, it is "the most precious part of our legal heritage." That heritage stands for two fundamental principles. One is that in the American political system the majority rules through electoral democracy. The other—expressed in the first ten Amendments—is that though we are a democracy, the rule of the majority must be limited so that individual liberty is guaranteed.

It is the second principle that people tend to forget or overlook. It is not as well understood as it ought to be. And it is very fragile, as many of the pages in this book demonstrate. Our rights are really limits on democratic power. They protect us from tyranny by the government itself. When citizens have the right to worship where and how they please, to organize political parties, and to distribute leaflets, it means the government has no legal authority to stop them. We saw the reasons why in the early chapters sketching the resistance of the English people and then the American colonists to unlimited power.

We've also seen how often the Bill of Rights is put to hard tests. Whenever America goes through a war or a fierce domestic conflict, our constitutional liberties are threatened. No matter whether it was the cold war between France and the United States in the early 1800s, the cold war between the Soviet Union and the United States in the twentieth century, the struggle over slavery in the nineteenth century, or the struggle over civil rights a hundred years later.

In such tense times a climate of fear and anger confuses the issues and blurs our perspective. When someone speaks out for the right of a person to voice an unpopular view, the defender of the First Amendment is accused of advocating that view. Forgotten is the idea that even in a democracy, just because one group commands more votes than another, it cannot be allowed to trample on the minority's rights.

The courts stand as safeguards against laws that go beyond the government's limited authority. The Supreme Court, above all, has the duty "to apply to ever changing conditions the never changing principles of freedom," as Justice Warren put it. There is, however, no assurance of steady growth. The range of constitutionally protected freedoms expands in some periods, contracts in others. The meaning of traditional freedoms changes as society changes in the course of history.

The Constitution, valued as highly as it is, is only a piece of paper. It does nothing by itself. The Bill of

Rights declares what our civil liberties are. But it does not carry out its commands. It takes the action of citizens to enforce our rights. Without an alert public, a critical press, and concerted political action, the safeguards our liberties provide can never be taken for granted.

TIME LINE

1215 MAGNA CARTA defines the law and limits the English king's power.

1628 PETITION OF RIGHT declares fundamental rights of Englishmen.

1649 AGREEMENT OF THE PEOPLE specifies rights Parliament cannot alter.

1656 Sir Henry Vane's "A HEALING QUESTION" proposes a people's convention to draw up a constitution.

1689 ENGLISH BILL OF RIGHTS states basic principles of liberty.

1689 THE TOLERATION ACT legalizes worship of Protestant nonconformists.

1765 Virginia colony adopts DECLARATION OF RIGHTS AND GRIEVANCES.

1765   Stamp Act Congress issues DECLARATION OF RIGHTS.

1772   Boston Town Meeting drafts DOCUMENT OF RIGHTS.

1774   First Continental Congress adopts DECLARATION OF RIGHTS.

1776   SECOND CONTINENTAL CONGRESS calls on colonies to set up their own governments. Each begins to draw up its own constitution, to include individual rights.

1787   Constitutional convention adopts U.S. CONSTITUTION, but without a Bill of Rights.

1789   Congress adopts federal BILL OF RIGHTS, as first ten amendments to the Constitution.

1791   Federal BILL OF RIGHTS ratified by the states.

1868   FOURTEENTH AMENDMENT to Constitution adopted. Its due process clause placed protection of federal government around rights that might be invaded by the states.

NOTE ON SOURCES

This is a list of sources I used in research. Readers wishing to follow up on some aspect of the general subject can look up the titles in the library. If your school or town library does not have a book you want, the librarian can usually borrow it for you through the interlibrary loan system.

Listed first and alphabetically are all the sources with author, title, publisher, and date given. Following the list are brief comments on titles of special importance, grouped by chapters. In this section I use the author's last name for easy reference to the bibliographic list.

BIBLIOGRAPHY

Anastoplo, George. *The Constitution of 1787: A Commentary.* Baltimore: Johns Hopkins, 1989.

Barth, Alan. *Law Enforcement Versus the Law.* New York: Collier, 1963.

Brant, Irving. *The Bill of Rights: Its Origin and Meaning.* Indianapolis: Bobbs-Merrill, 1965.

Burress, Lee. *Battle of the Books: Literary Censorship in the Public Schools, 1950–1985.* New York: Scarecrow, 1989.

Clayton, James E. *The Making of Justice: The Supreme Court in Action.* New York: Dutton, 1964.

Cohen, William, ed. *The Bill of Rights: A Source Book.* New York: Benziger, 1968.

Cox, Archibald. *The Court and the Constitution.* Boston: Houghton Mifflin, 1989.

Curry, Richard O. *Freedom at Risk: Secrecy, Censorship, and Repression in the 1980s.* Philadelphia: Temple, 1988.

Demac, Donna A. *Liberty Denied: The Current Rise of*

Censorship in America. New York: PEN American Center, 1988.

Dorman, Michael. *Witch Hunt: The Underside of American Democracy.* New York: Delacorte, 1976.

Dorsen, Norman, ed. *Our Endangered Rights.* New York: Pantheon, 1984.

Douglas, William P. *The Right of the People.* Garden City, NY: Doubleday, 1958.

Dumbauld, Edward. *The Bill of Rights and What It Means.* Westport, CT: Greenwood Press, 1957.

Fribourg, Marjorie. *The Bill of Rights.* New York: Avon, 1967.

Friedman, Lawrence M. *History of American Law.* New York: Simon & Schuster, 1985.

Gillespie, Michael Allen, and Michael Lemisch, eds. *Ratifying the Constitution.* Lawrence, KS: 1989.

Hand, Learned. *Bill of Rights.* Cambridge, MA: Harvard, 1958.

Journal of American History. Special Issue: "The Constitution and American Life." Vol. 74, No. 3, Dec. 1987.

Kammen, Michael. *A Machine That Would Go of Itself: The Constitution in American Culture.* New York: Knopf, 1986.

———. ed. *The Origins of the American Constitution.* New York: Penguin, 1986.

Kelly, Frank K. *Your Freedoms: The Bill of Rights.* New York: Putnam, 1964.

Kittrie, Nicholas N., and Eldon D. Wedlock, Jr., eds. *The Tree of Liberty.* Baltimore: Johns Hopkins, 1986.

Konvitz, Milton R., ed. *Bill of Rights Reader*. Ithaca, NY: Cornell, 1973.

Kurland, Philip B., ed. *Free Speech and Association: The Supreme Court and the First Amendment*. Chicago: University of Chicago Press, 1975.

Levy, Leonard W. *Constitutional Opinions: Aspects of the Bill of Rights*. New York: Oxford University Press, 1986.

———. *Emergence of a Free Press*. New York: Oxford University Press, 1987.

———. *Essays on the Making of the Constitution*. New York: Oxford University Press, 1987.

———. *Legacy of Suppression: Freedom of Speech and Press in Early American History*. Cambridge, MA: Harvard, 1960.

———. *Origins of the Fifth Amendment*. New York: Oxford University Press, 1968.

Lewis, Anthony. *Gideon's Trumpet*. New York: Random House, 1964.

Meltzer, Milton. *The Right to Remain Silent*. New York: Harcourt, 1972.

Miller, Arthur R. *Miller's Court*. Boston: Houghton Mifflin, 1982.

Neier, Aryeh. *Only Judgment: The Limits of Litigation in Social Change*. Middletown, CT: Wesleyan, 1982.

Padover, Saul K. *The Living U.S. Constitution*. New York: Mentor, 1983.

Rutland, Robert A. *The Birth of the Bill of Rights, 1776–1791*. Boston: Northeastern University Press, 1983.

Schwartz, Bernard, ed. *Roots of the Bill of Rights: An*

Illustrated Documentary History. 5 vols. New York: Chelsea House, 1980.

In addition to the sources listed above, I have made extensive use of articles in newspapers and periodicals bearing on recent issues affecting civil liberties, especially those reaching the U.S. Supreme Court for decision.

GENERAL BACKGROUND

The most valuable for this purpose is Schwartz's five-volume compilation of documents, dealing with the Bill of Rights from its English and colonial sources to its final ratification by the states. The editor's comments are as enlightening as the documents themselves. This work is often cited in Supreme Court decisions.

Brant analyzes the original concept of the Constitution and the way it has been interpreted throughout American history. He stresses that no plea of contemporary crisis must be allowed to curtail our freedoms. Fribourg covers much the same ground, but more briefly, with lively dramatization of important events. Cohen is designed for classroom use, to encourage discussion of principles basic to our freedoms. He examines current problems arising from application of the guarantees of the first ten amendments, provides references for teachers, and adds a table of important cases decided in the higher courts. Konvitz presents the major constitutional cases on Bill of Rights issues down to 1960. Friedman is a massive scholarly history that touches every conceivable aspect of law. It has long been a classic for students of law, history, and sociology. He shows how closely the law is interwoven with the nation's economic and political life. References to the Bill of Rights are frequent. Hand, one of the great American judges, is a brief essay, beautifully written and full of insights. Kelly is a concise and lucid exposition of the ten amendments, directed especially toward young people.

ORIGINS: CHAPTERS 1–7

Many of the sources given above deal with the origins of the Constitution and the Bill of Rights. In addition, all four of Levy's books provide incisive analyses of the development of the Bill of Rights. Varying points of view are offered in Gillespie, Kammen, and Rutland.

THE FIRST AMENDMENT: CHAPTERS 8–12

Freedom of religion and freedom of expression are the focus of the greatest attention in most of the vast literature on the Bill of Rights. Again, all the sources already listed go into the First Amendment. Dorman traces those congressional investigations he characterizes as witch-hunts from the first in 1792 down through the Nixon presidency. Curry demonstrates a connection in the 1980s between the obsession with secrecy and security and the violation of free expression. Demac, speaking for writers, weighs the considerable evidence of often successful attempts at censorship, and concludes that America is often as guilty of suppression as many other countries, in spite of the First Amendment. Kurland has provided a collection of scholarly essays from the annual *Supreme Court Review*, centering on First Amendment issues and the Supreme Court's interpretation of them.

CHAPTERS 13–18

Barth discusses the conflict between individual rights and law enforcement and provides the Supreme Court's interpretation of the Fourth and Fifth Amendments as of the time he wrote. Levy's book on the Fifth is now the classic source for the historical background of that amendment. Meltzer reviews briefly the origins of the Fifth and updates its application by the courts today. Lewis describes the Supreme Court case of *Gideon v. Wainwright* (1963) and explains the historical background of the right to counsel and the court's role in interpreting it. Dorsen gathers fifteen essays by leading experts of the American Civil Liberties Union that measure the ground gained or lost since the Warren Court years in the safeguarding of constitutional rights. Included are treatments of criminal justice, religion, national security, privacy, and racial, sexual, and economic justice. The book helps to clarify the dilemmas faced by lawmakers and the courts in today's world. Both Miller and Neier are provocative in their presentations of constitutional issues, challenging readers to decide what they think after hearing all sides of any given case.

INDEX

abolitionists, 80–82
abortion, 155–57
Adams, John, 6, 13, 33, 36, 75, 77, 78
Adams, Sam, 25, 26
Agreement of the People, 6, 15
Alabama, 82, 151
Alien and Sedition Acts, 75–79
American Civil Liberties Union, 141
American Revolution, 24–27, 147, 153
Anthony, Susan B., 110
Antifederalists, 39, 45
Articles of Confederation, 2, 34, 79

bail and fines, excessive, 62, 145–52
Bail Reform Bill, 146
Bill of Rights, American: as amendments, 41; colonial precedents, 10–21; English forerunners, 2–9; fragility, 159; ignorance of, ix-xii; as limits on power, 159; and natural law, 153–54; and omission from Constitution, 45; struggle for, 48–54; violated in Red Scares, 84–95. *See also* First Amendment, etc.
Bill of Rights, English, 7–9, 15, 25, 147
Black, Justice Hugo, 92, 141
blacklisting, 92
Blackmun, Justice Harry, 157
Borchard, Edwin M., 131
Brandeis, Justice Louis D., 126
Brennan, Justice William, 78
Brown, Edmund G., 148
Burger, Chief Justice Warren, 127, 143
Burress, Lee, 103

California, 148, 150
capital crimes, 58
Catholics, 12, 71
censorship, 56, 85, 96–107;
    abroad, 107; in schools,
    libraries, 99–105;
    opposition to, 104
Charles I, 5, 6, 15
Charles II, 19
Child, Lydia Maria, 81
Church, Frank, 98
civil liberties movement, 150,
    160
civil liberty defined, 29
civil rights movement, 113,
    150
Civil War, 51, 64, 110
Clark, Ramsey, 117
Coke, Sir Edward, 5, 25
Cold War, 86, 99, 112, 160
colonial charters, 10–21
Communism, 86–95, 112, 133
Connecticut, 54
Constitution of 1787, 2;
    amendment of, 41; drafting,
    37–47; and natural law,
    153–54; nature of framers,
    37–41; omission of Bill of
    Rights, 42; preamble, 43;
    publication, 45; ratifica-
    tion, 44–46; and slavery
    issue, 40
Constitutional amendments.
    See First Amendment, etc.
Constitutional conventions,
    33, 36–47
contraception, 155
Cotton, John, 16
cruel and unusual

punishment, 17, 145–52

death penalty, 148–50
Declaration of Independence,
    27, 31, 63, 109
Declaration of Rights and
    Grievances, 25
Delaware, 32, 45
Demac, Donna A., 102
domestic spying, 97
Donelson, Kenneth, 101
double jeopardy, 58–59
Douglas, Justice William O.,
    135, 153, 156, 157
Dred Scott decision, 82–83
due process of law, 4, 15,
    58–59

Eastland, James O., 90
Eighth Amendment, 62, 136,
    145–52
English Revolution, 23
equal protection of laws, 6, 16
Espionage Act, 85
exclusionary rule, 125

Federalists, 39, 40, 45, 54
Fellman, David, 113
Fifteenth Amendment, 64
Fifth Amendment, 26, 32,
    58–59, 129–35, 143, 156, 157
First Amendment, 20, 26, 27,
    51, 53, 55–56, 67–72, 73–83,
    91, 92, 94, 96–107, 109–14,
    129, 130, 133, 156, 157
Florida, 150
Fortas, Justice Abe, 141
Fourteenth Amendment,
    63–65, 123, 143, 157

Fourth Amendment, 26, 57–58, 122–28, 156, 157
Frankfurter, Justice Felix, 124
Franklin, Benjamin, 43–44
freedom of assembly, 26, 30, 55, 108–14
freedom of press, 30, 55, 73–83
freedom of religion, 6, 8–9, 17–19, 20, 26, 30, 32, 55, 67–72
freedom of speech, 16, 30, 55, 73–83
French and Indian War, 22

Garrison, William Lloyd, 81
George III, 31
Georgia, 33, 54, 81
Gerry, Elbridge, 42
Gideon, Clarence Earl, 141
Gideon v. Wainwright, 140–42
Goodman, Mark, 105
grand jury, 58–59
Griswold, Erwin, 135
Griswold v. Connecticut, 155–56
gun control, 115–20

habeas corpus, 43
Harlan, Justice John M., 128
Hatch Act, 155
Hazelwood v. Kuhlmeier, 104
Henry, Patrick, 6, 25, 89
heresy, 8, 17
Hofstadter, Richard, 71
Hollywood Ten, 91
Holmes, Ivan, 105
Hoover, J. Edgar, 86
House Un-American Activities Committee (HUAC), 89, 93

Illinois, 150
infamous crimes, 58
informers, 127
Inquisition, 8, 133

Jackson, Justice Robert H., 71
James I, 13, 18
Jay, John, 36
Jefferson, Thomas, 30–31, 32, 36, 48–49, 66, 71, 75, 77, 78, 89
Jehovah's Witnesses, 70, 71
Jews, 18, 71
John, King, 3
judicial review, 79–80

Kammen, Michael, 28, 40

Legal Aid Society, 142
Legal Services Corp., 142
Levellers, 7
Levy, Leonard, 74, 75, 132, 134
Lilburne, John, 134
Lincoln, Abraham, 66
Locke, John, 153
Lovejoy, Elijah, 82
Loyalty Program, 87–88

McCarthy, Joseph, 90, 93–94
McCarthyism, 87–95
McReynolds, Justice James C., 116
Madison, James, 2, 40, 71, 75; father of Constitution, 47, 48–54; framer of Bill of Rights, 2, 47; and judicial review, 79

Magna Carta, 2–5, 15, 16, 25, 109
Manhattan Bail Project, 146
Marbury v. Madison, 79, 82
Marshall, Chief Justice John, 79
Maryland, 15, 17, 32, 54
Mason, George, 29–31, 42
Massachusetts, 15–17, 33, 35, 54
Miranda, Ernesto, 143
Miranda v. Arizona, 143–44
Missouri Compromise, 82–83
Morris, Errol, 131
Morris, Gouverneur, 43
Morris, Richard B., 24
Murphy, Justice Frank, 124

National Rifle Association, 116
natural rights, 153–56
Nearing, Scott, 85
New Hampshire, 34, 46
New Jersey, 32
New Mexico, 152
New York, 33, 150
Nilsen, Aileen, 101
Nineteenth Amendment, 111
Ninth Amendment, 153–56, 158
Nixon Administration, 97
North Carolina, 32, 46

Otis, James, 6, 25

Palmer, A. Mitchell, 86
Penn, William, 19–20
Pennsylvania, 19–21, 32
Petition of Rights, 5, 15

Pogrebin, Letty Cottin, 117
political liberty, defined, 29
protection against search and seizure, 57
Puritans, 7, 15–17, 74, 134

Quakers, 18, 20, 100

Reagan Administration, 97, 142
Red Scares, 86–95
Rehnquist, Chief Justice William H., 149, 151
religion, teaching about, 68–70
reserved powers, 63, 157–58
reserved rights of people, 62
reserved rights of states, 63
Rhode Island, 17–19, 46
right against self-incrimination, 129–35
right of association, 108–14
right of privacy, 126, 153–57
right to bear arms, 56
right to counsel, 20, 60–61
right to be let alone, 121–28, 153–57
right to dissent, 73–95
right to organize, 111
right to participate in politics, 155
right to petition, 26, 30, 55
right to picket, 111–12
right to remain silent, 58–59, 129–35
right to trial by jury, 32, 60, 137
rights of prisoners, 150–52
rights of the accused, 58–59, 136–44

Roe v. Wade, 156–57
Roosevelt, Franklin D., 66

Schwartz, Bernard, 29, 52
Schwartz, Herman, 104
search and seizure, 123–28
Second Amendment, 56,
    115–20
seditious libel, 74–75
self-incrimination, 58–59
separation of church and
    state, 67–72
Seventh Amendment, 61,
    136–44
Shays's Rebellion, 35
Sherman, Roger, 42–52
Sixth Amendment, 21, 60–61,
    136–44
slavery, 17, 30, 31, 33, 40, 64,
    80–83, 110, 160
Smith, Margaret Chase, 93–94
Smith Act, 89
South Carolina, 33, 81
Stanford Law Review, 148
Stanton, Elizabeth Cady, 110
Stone, Chief Justice Harlan
    F., 158
Supreme Court, U.S., 65,
    79–80, 82–83, 89–92, 101,
    104, 111–13, 124–28, 137–44,
    147–51, 155–58

Taney, Chief Justice Roger
    B., 82
taxation, 4, 7, 24–26
Tennessee, 81
Tenth Amendment, 63,
    157–58
Texas, 150

Thin Blue Line, The, 131
Third Amendment, 57,
    121–22, 156
Thirteenth Amendment, 33,
    64, 110
Thomas, J. Parnell, 89
Tocqueville, Alexis de, 108
Toleration Act, 9
torture, 133
trial by jury, 4, 17, 19, 27, 42,
    43, 61
Truman, Harry, 87, 99

United States v. White, 127

Vane, Sir Henry, 7
Vera Foundation, 146
Vermont, 32, 33
Virginia, 10, 13, 14, 29–31, 46,
    53, 54
Vonnegut, Kurt, 104

Wagner Labor Relations Act,
    111
Ward, Nathaniel, 16
Warren, Chief Justice Earl,
    127, 159, 160
Washington, George, 30, 37,
    40, 46, 53, 71
Whittier, John Greenleaf, 82
Williams, Roger, 18
Wilson, Woodrow, 85
witch-hunts, 84–95
women's rights, 17, 110
World War I, 85
World War II, 86, 99, 101, 112,
    150

Zenger, John P., 74

ABOUT THE AUTHOR

Milton Meltzer has written over seventy-five books in the fields of history, biography, and social reform. His series on American ethnic groups for Thomas Y. Crowell includes *The Chinese Americans*; *The Hispanic Americans*; and *The Jewish Americans: A History in Their Own Words*, which was an ALA Notable Children's Book. His highly acclaimed *The Black Americans: A History in Their Own Words*, also an ALA Notable Children's Book, is newly revised and updated in a single-volume edition. In 1987 he edited *The American Revolutionaries: A History in Their Own Words 1750–1800*, which was an ALA Best Book for Young Adults. His most recent book for Harper & Row, *Rescue: The Story of How Gentiles Saved Jews in the Holocaust*, was also named both an ALA Best Book for Young Adults and a Notable Children's Book of 1988. His most recent book for Crowell is *Voices from the Civil War: A Documentary History of the Great American Conflict*.

His many other honors include five nominations for the National Book Award, most recently for *All Times, All Peoples: A World History of Slavery*, which also won the Christopher Award. Another title for Harper, *Ain't Gonna Study War No More: The Story of America's Peace Seekers*, was an ALA Notable Children's Book, an ALA Best Book for Young Adults, and the recipient of the Jane Addams Children's Book Award.

Mr. Meltzer was born in Worcester, Massachusetts, and educated at Columbia University. He is a member of the Authors' Guild. He lives with his wife in New York City. They have two daughters and a grandson.